THE LAST OF THE
NOMADS

The Last of the Nomads is the story of Warri and Yatungka, the last of the Mandildjara people to remain in their country — the Western Gibson Desert region of Western Australia.

After many years of drought — the worst this century — the Mandildjara held grave fears for the safety of Warri and Yatungka. Their chances of survival under such adverse conditions and without the support of younger tribesmen and women were extremely remote. So, at the request of the Aboriginal elders and with the guidance of Mudjon, an old friend of Warri's, Dr Peasley and his companions set out in search of the elderly couple.

Thus began an extraordinary journey, a journey into the past to locate a man and woman pursuing a nomadic existence, as their people had done since the dawn of human occupation of Australia. W J Peasley's account of the events of that journey, his description of the country and of the emotional meeting in the desert are fascinating, thoughtful and, at times, extremely moving.

The Last of the Nomads also provides an informative account of earlier Aboriginal habitation and the significance of the country to Aboriginal identity. A brief history of Wiluna, the famous Canning Stock Route and early European exploration, and an appreciation of Aboriginal-European relations help make this an important and absorbing book.

W J Peasley was born in the central west of New South Wales and spent his boyhood on his father's farm. There he was greatly excited by his discovery of ancient camp sites of Aboriginal people who had long since disappeared from the area. He was also saddened, for this was the only evidence left of a people who had occupied the land for thousands of years. About that time he read, for the first time, Henry Kendall's poem 'The Last of His Tribe' and this had a profound affect on him.

Leaving school at the age of fourteen, he worked on the family farm, in shearing sheds and as a drover's offsider. At the age of eighteen he enlisted in the 2nd AIF and was a member of the British Commonwealth Occupation Forces in Japan. After leaving the army he matriculated and studied medicine at the University of Sydney. On graduation he moved to Western Australia and for twelve years worked as a Flying Doctor in the North-West and Kimberley. There he was able to pursue his interest in Aboriginal culture and to witness many of the secret-sacred rites of the people.

Following several years in Europe he returned to Perth where he studied anthropology and continued his interest in Australian history, particularly the history of exploration, by embarking on several expeditions into the desert country, following the tracks of early explorers.

Married with four grown sons, Dr Peasley now lives in City Beach, Western Australia.

THE LAST OF THE
NOMADS

FREMANTLE PRESS
fine independent publishing

To my wife,
Anne

Introduction

This is the story of a journey into the heart of the Gibson Desert of Western Australia in search of an elderly Aboriginal couple, the last of their tribe remaining in their own 'country', the last of the Aboriginal people left in the Western Gibson Desert and possibly the last nomads on the Australian continent to follow the way of life of their ancestors.

For my companions and I, it was a journey into the past, to locate and observe a man and woman pursuing a nomadic existence, as their people had done since the dawn of human occupation of Australia.

In an age when man travels faster than the speed of sound, when he can both hear and see events happening on the other side of the world the moment they occur, where he has journeyed to the moon and returned, an aged Aboriginal man and his wife were still living amongst the sandhills of the Western Australian desert, completely oblivious to all these wondrous things and with little knowledge of the world beyond the horizon.

They were thought to be hunting and food gathering over the land as their fathers had done before them, unaware of, and uninterested in the happenings of the outside world. War, famine, revolution, acts of terrorism, things of great moment for civilisation meant nothing to that man and woman. On the infrequent occasions when outsiders had made contact with them in recent years they had never expressed any interest in life outside their own land, their 'country'.

Why did this couple, the very last of their tribe, choose to live alone in the desert? To answer this question it is necessary to examine the history, the sad history, of the Aboriginal people of Australia since the beginning of European occupation of the land.

This story was written following many requests from people wishing to know more about a unique Aboriginal man and woman; their reasons for remaining alone in the desert, the lifestyle they followed and their reactions to the white man's world. It was also written in an attempt to answer some of the criticism levelled at us by people who, not having full knowledge of the facts, laboured under many misconceptions.

There were those who loudly denounced us for bringing the couple out of the desert. It was said they should have been left to pursue their way of life unpolluted by 'civilisation', that we had no right to intrude, that it was far better they be left to die in the desert in their own 'country', than to live the degrading existence of the fringe dwellers.

Those critics will, I trust, be answered satisfactorily in this book, where the full facts are recorded for the first time. Without knowledge of the events leading up to the meeting out in the Gibson Desert, of the appalling conditions in which the couple were forced to live in the worst drought of the century it was, I suppose, understandable that some criticism should have been directed at us. Of our critics however I would ask two questions. What manner of man or woman would refuse to undertake a search when requested by Aboriginal elders, desperately anxious about the safety of two of their kinsfolk?

Who, after undertaking a long search and finding them alive but emaciated and ill, without adequate food and water, would be prepared to leave them in the desert to die alone? For death was not far away at Ngarinarri.

Left: Warri Kyangu of the Mandildjara.

Above: Yatungka of the Mandildjara.

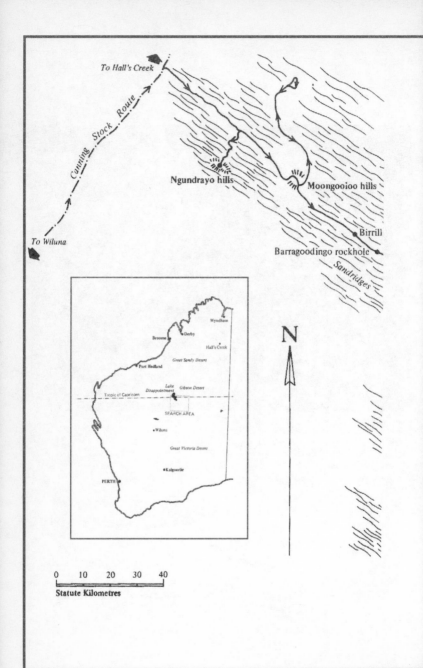

To Hall's Creek

Cunning Stock Route

To Wiluna

Ngundrayo hills

Moongooioo hills

Birrill

Barragoodingo rockhole

Sandridges

N

Wyndham

Broome

Derby

Hall's Creek

Great Sandy Desert

Port Hedland

Tropic of Capricorn

Lake Disappointment

Gibson Desert

SEARCH AREA

Wiluna

Great Victoria Desert

Kalgoorlie

PERTH

0   10   20   30   40
Statute Kilometres

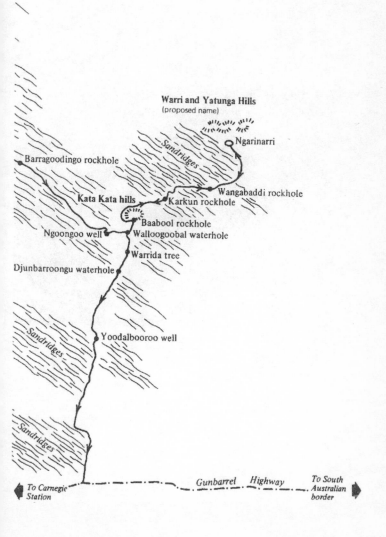

Route taken by the search expedition.

Warri and Yatunga Hills
(proposed name)

Sandridges

Ngarinarri

Barragoodingo rockhole

Wangabaddi rockhole

Kata Kata hills

Karkun rockhole

Baabool rockhole

Ngoongoo well

Walloogoobal waterhole

Warrida tree

Djunbarroongu waterhole

Sandridges

Yoodalbooroo well

Sandridges

To Carnegie Station

Gunbarrel Highway

To South Australian border

Chapter One

The occupation of the Australian mainland began more than forty thousand years ago but, contrary to popular belief, there has never been a complete land bridge between the southern continent and Asia. To reach Australian shores would have entailed a hazardous journey across open sea. Even during the Ice Ages, when the sea fell to its lowest levels, the distance that had to be traversed was more than eighty kilometres. It would have required great courage to embark on such a perilous venture across unknown waters with the nearest land mass to the south hidden from view below the horizon.

The oceans of the world were at their lowest levels (up to one hundred and forty metres below present-day levels) some ninety thousand, seventy thousand, fifty-five thousand, thirty-five thousand and eighteen thousand years ago, and these would have been the most suitable times for any crossing from the island chain in the north to the Australian mainland. There is evidence to indicate that man was already well established on the continent before the low sea levels of thirty-five thousand years ago. Had he arrived during the previous Ice Age some twenty thousand years earlier?

A long-disused Aboriginal ceremonial ground on the southern fringe of the Gibson Desert, the significance of which is uncertain.

The oldest human occupation sites that have been discovered in Australia are located in the southern half of the mainland. Does this indicate that the original inhabitants landed on the southern shore? This would appear to be highly improbable. I would suggest that there are far more ancient sites to be found in northern Australia, particularly the closest point to the northern island chain. However it must be borne in mind that the archaeological evidence which could possibly shed much light on the question of the location of the first landings, lies today far below the surface of the Arafura Sea.

If the first human visitors did, in fact, come ashore in the Kimberley region they would have found a relatively fertile land with a high rainfall. Food and water would have been readily available and for a very long period of time there would not have been any population pressures to necessitate a movement across the less fertile country to the south. Yet there were Aboriginal people living in the southern part of the continent forty thousand years ago. It has been suggested that within the space of some two thousand years, the descendants of the original immigrants had occupied the whole of the Australian mainland. This is difficult to believe for, as stated previously, there would not have been any pressures on the people to bring about such a rapid infiltration to every corner of the land.

I believe that a much greater period of time elapsed before the Aboriginal people penetrated to every corner of Australia. With the discovery of occupation sites in the south dating back forty thousand years and, presuming that a time period of ten to twenty thousand years was required for the inhabitants to reach those sites, one can postulate that the first landing occurred between fifty and fifty-five thousand years ago. This was the time of the previous Ice Age, when the ocean level was at its lowest point, a time when a sea crossing was most likely to occur.

There is evidence to show that there have been several waves of immigrants and they probably took place at the time of the Ice Ages of the thirty-five thousand and eight thousand years ago. The Aboriginal people do not speak a common language as one would expect if their ancestors had a common origin. There are, or were, between three hundred and five hundred different languages and dialects, and in some areas, such as the Kimberley, the language spoken by adjacent tribal groups is so different that it appears obvious the ancestors of the people came from different places and possibly arrived at different times.

The theory of several waves of immigrants is further supported by the fact that the dingo, the native dog, did not appear on the continent until somewhere between seven thousand and ten thousand years ago and, as there was no land bridge over which this animal could migrate to Australia, it could only have been transported across the sea by humans. That there were no dingoes on the continent prior to that time is indicated by the absence of remains older than about five thousand years and the fact that they did not exist in Tasmania. The rising sea levels after the last Ice Age separated the island from the mainland between ten thousand and twelve thousand years ago, before the dingo had penetrated to the southernmost parts of the land.

Where did the Aboriginal people of Australia come from? There has been a great deal of conjecture as to their origin. Some evidence points to the possibility of a migration of people from central and southern India down the island chain that extended to the south from Asia. The physical features of the Dravidians of India in many ways bear a striking resemblance to those of many Australian Aborigines, while the use of the throwing weapon, the boomerang, by both peoples and the similarity of the language structure in some cases suggests that at least some of the Aboriginal people may have had Dravidian ancestors. Small pockets of people possessing some of the characteristics of both Dravidians and Aborigines are to be found along the island chain, perhaps the remnant of a southerly migration of long ago.

The main objection to the Dravidian–Australian Aborigine theory is the fact that the blood groupings of the people of Southern India are dissimilar to those of present-day Aborigines, although an attempt has been made to explain this as being the result of the great demographic changes that have taken place in India during the last fifty thousand years.

Whatever their origin, the first human arrivals in Australia, after establishing themselves in their new land, began to gradually spread over the vast continent until by the year 1788, when the first European settlement was established, there were an estimated three hundred thousand Aboriginal people scattered across the country. They were divided into about five hundred different tribal groups.

At this point, it is important to remember that Aborigines had, at that time, occupied the whole of the Australian mainland and the island of Tasmania. Every square yard of Australian soil was owned by, and was of very great significance to, one tribal group or another. Each group lived within their own tribal boundaries believing that their tract of land, their 'country' had been delineated in the far distant past, in the Dreamtime.

There was considerable movement across these boundaries for reasons of social intercourse, trade and ceremonial activities, but little evidence is available to indicate that tribal borders were crossed by people bent on acquiring new territory by conquest. Aboriginal people believed that their particular area of land was theirs and theirs alone. It could not be taken from them and they in turn, could not annex country that belonged to others. They were responsible for the protection and maintenance of the sacred sites within their territory, but could only visit the sacred sites of their neighbours by invitation.

The land was the very essence of their being. It had been entrusted to them by the creators at the Dreamtime. They were born of the spirits that inhabited the land and they knew that on their death they would return to the soil to await rebirth. They could not leave and take up residence anywhere else, for to live away from their country was to live without substance. The world was meaningless without the spiritual bond of their own land.

Because Aboriginal people were so deeply bonded to their country they could not retreat before the advancing settlements of the Europeans. They lacked the numbers and the organisation to resist the invaders and within a few short years the tribes that occupied the coastal regions largely disappeared. Their sacred sites were despoiled by the colonists, their land was taken from them, they were prevented from hunting over territory that had been theirs since the Dreamtime, and they were punished for infringements of the white man's laws, laws that they could not comprehend.

A grinding stone on a dry claypan.

Not only did they lose possession of their land, their way of life was also ridiculed and their social structure was undermined. They contracted the diseases introduced by the white man, against which they had no immunity. They wandered about aimlessly or huddled on the fringes of the settlements, and they lost the will to live, for without their land, their heritage from the Dreamtime, there was no meaning to life.

However, some Aboriginal people were fortunate. The white men were only interested in occupying the land that could be cultivated or would support their livestock. Their advance over the country was halted by the great deserts of inland Australia, which were to become the last stronghold of traditional Aboriginal life. In those areas, the people were free to live as they had done since the Dreamtime, with little interference from the outside world.

The Gibson Desert of Western Australia was one such place. A vast, ill-defined stretch of country, the Gibson extends from the Rawlinson Ranges in the east to Lake Disappointment, hundreds of kilometres away to the west. In the north it merges with the Great Sandy Desert and, in the south, with the Great Victoria Desert. It is a great expanse of sandhills running parallel to the horizon, of huge open spinifex plains and belts of mulga trees and low scrub. There are few geographical features to relieve the monotony of the landscape. No mountains of any significance rise out of the plains, no rivers flow through the land. As one moves across the desert, occasional low hills and breakaways appear on the horizon, the eroded remains of mountain ranges of long ago. In places, the surface is covered with fine gravel, 'the great undulating desert of gravel', described by the Honourable David Carnegie during his epic crossing of the Gibson in 1896.

The desert was named by Ernest Giles, the courageous explorer, after his companion Alfred Gibson who, in 1874, lost his life whilst attempting to cross the arid country from South Australia to the west coast. In his journal, Giles wrote:

> *I called this terrible region that lies between the Rawlinson Ranges and the next permanent water that may eventually be found to the west, Gibson desert, after the first white victim to its horrors.*

But this arid 'terrible region' which, to the white man is inhospitable, a place to be feared, was once the home of many Aboriginal tribes: the Budidjara, the Gadudjara, the Mandildjara, the Ngadadjara, the Wanman and others. They were not afraid of the desert, it was their country, a land like no other. They were as one with the rocks, the dry creeks, the rock holes that were created long ago by Wati Kudjara, the two mythical men whose work could be seen at every turn. By their very isolation these tribes were able to maintain their traditional way of life while their people in the more fertile areas, who bore the brunt of the white man's invasion, were powerless to prevent the destruction of their society.

The people of the Gibson spoke a common tongue, the language of the Western Desert, and they had little contact with the outside world prior to the early 1900s. Their country had been crossed by the exploration parties of Warburton (1873), Forrest (1874), Giles (1876), Wells (1896) and Carnegie (1896). An occasional prospecting expedition penetrated their land but found little of geological interest. Then, in the early years of the twentieth century a series of permanent wells were established across the desert from Wiluna to Halls Creek, a distance of one thousand six hundred kilometres. It was now possible for cattle to travel from the Kimberley to the railhead at Wiluna across formerly waterless country, and this was to have a significant effect on the desert people. They now had a sure water supply from the white man's wells and they made contact with the parties of drovers who pushed their herds of cattle south across the desolate land. Their isolation was beginning to break down. A movement out of the desert began and this rapidly gained momentum, and once having left their tribal land, few of the Aboriginal people returned to their homeland.

In the 1950s and 1960s small groups of the remnants of several tribes were still wandering over their lands. The policy of the Government at that time was to encourage those that remained in the desert to settle in the mission stations and reserves on the fringes of the settlements. Many were transported by land and by air to be 'civilised'. Many, too, came out of the desert without any encouragement, drifting into the settled areas, following a pattern that had been going on in other places for more than one hundred and fifty years.

For those who chose to remain in their own land, life became increasingly difficult. They were the older generation who did not display the same curiosity in the white man's ways as the younger members of the tribes. A great burden was placed on those who were left, for there were not sufficient numbers of young men and women to support the old.

As a result of their depleted numbers it became impossible for the Aborigines to sustain their social structure, to perform the rites of passage and to engage in the increase ceremonies that were required to ensure that animals and birds multiplied and the rains fell.

If a man wished to obtain a wife it was necessary for him to travel out of the desert to the settled areas where large numbers of his kinsfolk had chosen to live. Tribal law dictated that a man might not marry before he had passed through his initiation and this process was a long one. It was necessary for him to remain away from his country for a long period and many did not return home again after they had assumed the status of a man.

By the mid 1970s the drift that had begun only a few short years previously was almost complete. The country of the Budidjara, the Gadudjara, the Ngadadjara and the Wanman was empty, devoid of any human inhabitants. For the first time in possibly twenty thousand years, there were no Aboriginal people ranging across these tribal lands.

But the land of the Mandildjara had not been completely deserted by its people. Two people remained to hunt and gather food across their country, as their ancestors had done before them. They were the very last of their people, the last of the nomads.

Chapter Two

Warri Kyangu and his wife, Yatungka, of the Mandildjara, chose
to remain in their ancestral land in the Gibson Desert when their
kinsfolk moved out to the missions and settlements of the white
man. They did so for two reasons. There was that deep love for
their own land, their 'country', which was far more than a piece
of real estate to them. They were bonded to the soil, it was an
essential part of their existence. A non-Aboriginal has always had
great difficulty in comprehending this intense relationship, and
this lack of understanding continues to the present day.

Secondly, they feared the retribution that would be sought by
the elders should they rejoin their people. Long ago they had
committed a grave breach of tribal law. They had disregarded the
rules of marriage of their people, a serious offence indeed.
Although many years had passed since they had broken the law
they knew the old men had not forgotten. The punishment for
their offence had never been exacted for a number of reasons.

The system of marriage into which Warri and Yatungka had
been born allowed a man who belonged to a particular section of
the tribe to choose, or be allotted, a wife from another section.
He could not marry a woman from the same section as himself or

from a section which belonged to the same half, or moiety.

If there are four sections A, B, C, D, these are divided into two halves, or moieties A C and B D.

Section A	Section B
Section C	Section D
(moiety A – C)	(moiety B – D)

A man of section A would normally marry a woman of section B. This is the preferred marriage, but not all women of B are available to him. He cannot, for example, take for a wife any females of B who are already married, nor any of B who are related to him.

If none in section B are available or suitable he can choose a spouse from section D. This is the alternative marriage and is acceptable within the marriage rules of the tribe.

A man of A marrying a woman of B would have children who would belong to D. The male children would then marry females of C, or alternatively, of A.

A man of A would, under no circumstances, be allowed to marry a woman of his own section or from the other section in his moiety, C. Likewise a man of B could not marry a woman of B or D, but would choose from A (preferred) or C (alternative). In the case of the Mandildjara people section A is known as Yiparka, B is Djararu, C is Burungu and D is Milanjga.

YIPARKA	DJARARU
BURUNGU	MILANJGA

Warri was born a Yiparka, being the son of a Burungu woman who had married a Milanjga man. His preferred marriage was with a Djararu woman and their children would be Milanjga, the section of his father.

But the woman that Warri chose was not a Djararu or even of the Milanjga. She was Yatungka, born a Burungu, the same section as his mother and in the same moiety as himself. This union would never be condoned by the elders. Yatungka was to be the wife of a Milanjga. Warri knew he could not take her as his wife and remain with his people. He could suppress his desire for her, adhere to the law and marry a Djararu, or he could take Yatungka and flee from his country. He chose the latter course, and having made that momentous decision he and his new wife crept away from the camp as the people slept.

Warri and Yatungka were aware that a punitive party would follow in the hope of apprehending them and escorting them back to their country to face the judgement of the elders. He and Yatungka moved quickly to place as much distance as possible between them and their expected pursuers.

The elders, having discovered that the couple had eloped, met to discuss the course of action that was to be followed. A man was selected to follow the trail, to force the wrongdoers to return and allow the law to take its course. That man was Mudjon. Short in stature but strong in body, he had impressed his people by his great powers of endurance, his hunting skills and his adherence to the laws of his ancestors.

He and Warri had been close friends. They had played together as children, later they had passed through their initiation together, and as men they had hunted across the plains. The task that Mudjon had now been ordered to undertake was, in consequence, not one that he relished. He was to hunt down his old friend and command him to return to his people. If Warri resisted, force was to be used.

Mudjon followed the eloping couple away to the south-west. He noted from their tracks that Warri and Yatungka had moved rapidly, intent on establishing a great lead on those who would follow. They knew they would not be safe until they were far outside their own country and far from their own people.

They reached the low hills of Kata Kata and turned to the north-west to enter the land of the Budidjara. Mudjon followed, past Paragoodingu rock hole and on towards the permanent water at Moongooloo. Early one morning he cautiously approached a waterhole situated in an area of low gravelly undulations, with scattered mulga trees providing shelter for anyone camping near the water. This was the rock hole known as Birrill, deep in Budidjara country.

Mudjon was cautious, for he had seen smoke rising above the trees as he walked towards Birrill. Creeping forward over a rise he saw a group of Budidjara men, women and children seated close to the rock hole and amongst them Warri and Yatungka, who appeared to have established a friendly relationship with them.

For Mudjon this meant that in apprehending the couple he would risk being attacked, not only by Warri but by the men of the Budidjara as well. However, he had been sent on a mission by the elders and he must carry out his orders, whatever the obstacles, whatever the difficulties he might encounter.

Gathering his spears together he strode briskly into the clearing near the waterhole and challenged Warri to come forward with Yatungka and accompany him back to Mandildjara country. The reply came in the form of a shower of spears thrown by Warri and the Budidjaras. Mudjon deflected several of these missiles with his shield and threw several in return. No injuries were sustained by any of the participants in this exchange. There was much shouting and gesticulating, threats and insults were hurled, but Mudjon stood his ground and demanded that Warri be delivered up to him. The request was refused and once more spears rained down about the lone figure.

Gradually the posturing and shouting subsided and Mudjon warily moved in closer to talk to Warri and Yatungka, to persuade them to leave the Budidjara people and return home to face the judgement of the elders. Warri, however, was adamant in his refusal. He wanted Yatungka to remain as his wife and declared he would not give her up under any circumstances. He would not go back to Mandildjara country for he feared that, not only would he be severely punished for his breach of law but also that his woman would be taken from him, punished and then claimed by the man to whom she had been promised.

Warri and Yatungka slipped away from Birrill that night, fleeing far to the west. Mudjon knew it would be useless to follow any further and sadly he retraced his steps back to his own country, there to report to the elders on the failure of the mission that had been entrusted to him. He was sad because he had lost a good friend in Warri, his hunting companion of former years. Sad too because Warri had deliberately broken the law, something that was unthinkable to Mudjon, for adherence to the law and the ways of his ancestors was of paramount importance to him. In his mind, the rules that had been formulated in the Dreamtime were to be obeyed at all times. If the law was not upheld the Mandildjara would not survive.

Warri and Yatungka remained in exile for a great many years. Children were born to them, fine strong sons, but happiness eluded them. They were outside their own country and no Mandildjara man or woman could be happy if they were unable to wander the land of their birth, to hunt and gather food and to participate in the social gatherings and sacred rituals of their people. They were exiles, living in a strange land, amongst strange people.

The time came when the feeling for their country became too strong to bear, their sadness so profound that they chose to return and face the consequences. With their children they travelled back across the spinifex plains and sandhills until once more they stood in the land of the Mandildjara. What would their reception be amongst their own people? What punishment would be inflicted upon them?

Warri and Yatungka found that great changes had occurred during their absence. There had been an exodus of people from the desert. They had returned to a land that was almost empty. Remnants of the Mandildjara tribe still wandered their country in small family groups, but there was little social organisation to ensure that the law was upheld.

Warri and Yatungka were not punished for their defiance of the marriage rules. There was no body of elders left to pass judgement on such matters. The couple, with their children, became just another family unit moving up and down their ancestral land. They were home but it was not the home they had known before fleeing into exile.

No longer would Warri join the other men to hunt the *malu* (kangaroo), the *djakapiri* (emu) and the *papa nguyama* (dingo). No longer would Yatungka wander with the women, as they foraged for edible roots or caught small reptiles or collected seeds to be ground into flour. No longer would there be large gatherings round the camp fires when groups of children played, the young people sang and the older men and women discussed the hunt or reminisced about events of days gone by. There were no more ceremonies to mark the passage of boys into manhood. All this belonged to the past in the Gibson Desert.

In the years that followed their homecoming, Warri and Yatungka saw their remaining kinsfolk leave their country for the attractions of the white man's world. As their own children became adults they too were forced to leave, to travel to the south for initiation and to seek wives, and they chose to remain there, occasionally returning to their homeland for brief visits.

The time came when Warri and Yatungka were the only human occupants of the Mandildjara land and indeed of the vast expanse of the Western Gibson Desert. They alone were left to wander as their ancestors had done for centuries, moving from one waterhole to another, hunting and food gathering, two people alone in the desert.

When the rains fall and the seasons are good, there is an abundance of water in the soaks and rock holes, game is plentiful and life is not difficult for the people of the desert. But when the rains do not come the vegetation withers away, the waterholes dry up and game becomes scarce, and it is only with a great deal of effort that sufficient food and water for daily needs can be obtained.

Under these circumstances, when the large family groups moved about the country, it was the young men and women of the Mandildjara who travelled great distances in the daily search for edibles. In this way sufficient food could usually be obtained to support the old and infirm who were incapable of foraging in such a manner. Without the young, life could be hard for the elderly when the rains did not come to the desert.

Warri and Yatungka, the lone survivors in the desert, were placed in such a position. For three years little rain had fallen, a great drought had descended upon their land. The waterholes gradually dried up, animal and bird life perished or moved away to more hospitable regions. The last of the desert Mandildjara people were in great danger of death from thirst or starvation. Their kinsmen away to the south, aware of the extreme conditions of drought that prevailed in their country, became increasingly anxious. Daily they scanned the sky to the north for some sign that rain might fall on their homeland. They searched in vain, and feared for the safety of the old couple. The only evidence to indicate they were still wandering the Mandildjara country, that they might be alive, was a report of a 'smoke' having been seen in that area in 1976.

The old men were convinced this was a signal sent up by Warri, for who else was out there to fire the country? A search must be made for Warri and Yatungka, they said. They must be found and, if they were still alive, be given help as soon as possible, said the elders, who themselves had lived in the desert and knew how difficult it was to survive a long drought. If the old couple were still alive they could not possibly live through another summer without rain. A search party must go, and go quickly, before the onset of the hot season.

In the late winter of 1976 I was a member of a small party which penetrated deep into the Gibson Desert. We had sighted 'smoke' on the horizon, which appeared to come from the Mandildjara country. It was a great distance off and shortage of fuel prevented us from investigating at that time. On our return to Wiluna we reported our observation to the old Aboriginal men who considered that only Warri and Yatungka could have made the smoke. In 1977, because no rain had fallen in the desert, the old men approached a member of our party, Stan Gratte, who was on a visit to Wiluna, and suggested that we institute a search for Warri and Yatungka. We had been planning another journey into the Western Desert which would take us far to the north of Mandildjara country. That plan must be abandoned, said the old men, for it was imperative that Warri and Yatungka be found within the next few weeks. They argued their case so vigorously and expressed their fears so strongly that we finally agreed to their request. We would mount an expedition to the Gibson Desert, with all possible speed, to search for the last of the nomads.

Chapter Three

In August 1977 our small party assembled in the little town of Wiluna. It consisted of five white men: Mr Stan Gratte, Dr John Hanrahan, Mr Harry Lever, Mr Mark Whittome and myself, and one Aborigine, Mudjon. Our transport was to be three four-wheel drive vehicles: a Toyota Land Cruiser, a Range Rover and a Land Rover.

Wiluna was chosen as the starting point for our expedition. It lies below the southern fringe of the Gibson Desert and for many years has been the home of Mudjon and many former desert dwellers. With a population of about fifty white people and several hundred Aborigines it is a mere shadow of its former self. Of the many hotels that once did a flourishing trade in the town's heyday only one remains to cater for the thirst of the residents. There is a police station staffed by two police officers and one Aboriginal aide, a post office, a nursing post and a co-operative store, run by the Aboriginal community.

There are a few scattered houses that are still occupied but much of the old town has been demolished or allowed to sink into a state of disrepair.

In 1892 the explorer, L A Wells, discovered auriferous country in the area and the gold rush that resulted was instrumental in the establishment of a town near Lake Way (also discovered and named by Wells). The settlement was first known as Lake Way but in 1897 this was changed to Wiluna, supposedly the Aboriginal word *Weeloona* (place of wind). Over the years, there has been considerable controversy as to the origin of the name.

The new town flourished and its discoverer, Wells, found a thriving community of over seven thousand people when he visited the place in 1935. There were several hotels doing a brisk trade with the miners and prospectors. A grassed playing field stood out vividly in the red-brown landscape. The townspeople were proud of their Olympic-sized swimming pool and the tennis courts that were illuminated at night, and they boasted of one of the most modern mining plants in Australia.

Wells saw the town at its height, for within a few years it was to fall into a rapid decline and in 1947, with the closure of the mine, the death knell for Wiluna was sounded. The majority of the population moved out, buildings were demolished or shuttered and today there is little to indicate that there was once a thriving 'Outpost of the Empire' on the edge of the desert.

Today the Weeloona Hotel, once the scene of many wild binges as the prospectors celebrated their successes or drowned their sorrows, stands deserted on the main street. One of the many hotels accredited with having the longest bar in Australia, it closed its doors long ago. Today the only sound is the wind as it whistles through the cracks and half-open doors, where once the raucous voices of drinkers echoed through the building. A mound of hay has replaced the long bar, ready tinder for any drunk that may stagger in to sleep off his overindulgence. Sadly the old hotel is to be demolished for reasons of safety but until that day arrives the inscription on the facade high above the street continues to announce to all who pass that way that it is the 'Weeloona Hotel'.

Wiluna, despite the exodus of the population, did not suffer the fate of so many of the mining towns in Western Australia. It did not become a ghost town. There was an influx of Aboriginal people from the desert who established their camps in the vicinity. The newcomers gathered together in tribal groups and initially the traditional culture was maintained. But they were now subjected to strong influences they had never encountered in the desert. The materialism of the white man's culture, the white man's denigration of Aboriginal beliefs and lifestyle and, above all, the destructive effects of alcohol, which in a few years was the major factor in the disintegration of the society of the desert people.

The Aboriginal people of Australia, unlike most other races, had never developed any form of alcoholic beverage. As a result, their culture had never been geared to the use of alcohol and to the social effects of its abuse. There were no rules laid down in the Dreamtime to control its use. The tribal elders had no guidelines to assist them and, having no precedents from their totemic ancestors, they lacked authority to formulate the necessary rules.

Today there are few of the Aboriginal people of Wiluna who do not take alcohol in excess. Why has this happened? Perhaps the absence of any traditional controls over the use of alcohol may be only a minor aetiological factor. One of the major contributing factors is the loss of identity which has been brought about by continual denigration of their culture and the persecution of their people for almost two hundred years. A second factor follows on from this loss of identity. They lack of any hope of re-establishing themselves as a people with their own culture, the feeling of hopelessness that saps the energy, the utter boredom that settles on the community. To drink alcohol to excess and to seek oblivion is an escape from the realities of fringe-dwelling life.

Aboriginal elders who have been entrusted with the maintenance of the traditional way of life are saddened as they watch their people abandon the culture of their ancestors. They see the law being broken at every turn. The social organisation is disintegrating before their eyes and they sometimes despair of the future. They attempt to instil in the young the knowledge that has been handed down to them. They perform the initiation rites for the young men, and organise the ceremonies that are an integral part of Aboriginal life. They desperately hope that their culture and their law will not be lost but they see little interest being shown by the young. The elders say, 'You cannot drink and follow the law', for a man under the influence of alcohol may talk and in talking may reveal to those who should not hear the secrets that have been handed down to him. They will only select for initiation those they consider will hold true to the law, such candidates becoming fewer and fewer as the years pass by. What has happened elsewhere in Australia appears to be happening in Wiluna. The custodians of the secrets of the Aboriginal people, the tribal elders, may one day feel that there are none to whom they can safely pass on the secret knowledge, with the result that the culture of the desert people will gradually disappear as the old men die. Should this happen, it will be a tragedy for the Aboriginal people and for Australia.

Chapter Four

Mudjon of the Mandildjara is one of the elders engaged in the task of bringing his people back to their traditional beliefs and away from the world of the white man, a world which many of the desert people cannot fully comprehend. He fervently believes that if the Aboriginal people hold to their culture and if they adhere to the law of their ancestors, there is hope that they will be able to stand alone. They will have a strong sense of identity, they will gain their self-respect and can then show the white man that the desert people have a culture and a way of life for which they need apologise to none.

Mudjon is prepared to lead his people away from the town, to take them back into the desert, back to their own country where they can renew their relationship with their land. But how many would follow? How many would turn their backs on the things that the white man values and which they, too, have come to value? The white man's food, the clothing, the transistor radios, the record players and above all, the white man's drink. Mudjon believes there are many who would be willing to forsake these things, but there are few who share his opinion.

Mudjon was to accompany us in the search for Warri and

Yatungka, because the country we would be traversing was that over which he had wandered with his people. Every detail of this land was known to him, from the low hills of Bulgarri, Tjurina and Wanderandja in the east to Djunderoo soak in the west. From Djulinoo soak in the south to beyond Yallendjiri rock hole in the north, he was familiar with every well and rock hole, every geographical feature. And Mudjon had wandered far outside his own country and was familiar with much of the Gibson Desert. As a young man he had roamed the Budidjara land to the west. He had visited the Ngadadjara in the south. He had gone into the country of the Pitjandjara, the Pintubi and the Walpiri. He had travelled far, and what he saw he never forgot.

Mudjon had first seen white men and women when he was on 'walkabout' to the Warburton Ranges. A mission had been established there in the early 1930s and for many of the desert people this was their first contact with non-Aborigines. Mudjon observed the missionaries from a distance. He noted their strange behaviour and heard them speak in a strange tongue. He feared them for he had heard his people speak of the terrible things that had been done by the white man, the atrocities committed against Aboriginal people when they had speared the cattle that had spread out over the land, land that belonged to them, their land since the Dreamtime.

In the early 1950s, a great gathering of tribes from the desert and settlements was planned. The venue was to be a place below the southern fringe of the desert, a place which had long been the traditional meeting ground of the Aboriginal people but which was now claimed by white man as his own.

Much organisation was necessary before the meeting could be held and messengers were despatched to travel far and wide; into the desert, to the pastoral communities and to the missions and settlements to summon all Aboriginal people to what was to be a momentous gathering.

Mudjon, elder of the Mandildjara people.

Mudjon, in company with many others of his people who were still wandering their land, heard of the proposed meeting and made the long journey south. He was apprehensive. He knew he was moving into white man's country and he believed there was much truth in the stories he had been told long ago by his father.

Several hundred Aboriginal people gathered at the meeting place. There was much singing and dancing, much laughter and gossip. Hunting parties were organised to ensure a supply of food for the multitude. There were also serious discussions amongst the elders and far-reaching decisions were made. They considered that it was not possible to maintain a viable social structure amongst the few who remained in the desert. If the Aboriginal people were to survive as a group they could only do so if all lived in close proximity to one another, for without sufficient numbers their society, their culture, would disintegrate.

Several men who were present at the meeting were delegated to go back into the desert and persuade the few who remained there to move south and join their kinsfolk. Mudjon was chosen to make contact with those who still wandered the Mandildjara country. He undertook the long walk back to the north and moving from waterhole to waterhole, gathered the little family groups together, amongst them being Warri and Yatungka with their young children. Mudjon was to lead them out of the desert to what he and others of his people believed was to be a better life.

The little group moved slowly southwards, following an invisible path that their people had travelled for centuries. Past the waterholes of Wangabaddi and Karkun and on to Kata Kata and Walloogoobal and Djunbabingo.

Mudjon noticed that as the party moved further and further to the south Warri became increasingly apprehensive. Every step in that direction brought him closer to the judgement of his people. One night when they were camped a little to the south of Yudalburoo rock hole, Warri and Yatungka and their children slipped away into the darkness. At dawn when Mudjon noted their absence the little family was far away. He followed the tracks for a short distance but there was nothing to be gained in proceeding further. Warri and Yatungka were heading north at great speed, back to their own country and away from civilisation and the retribution of the elders.

Mudjon and his group continued south into the white man's land. Some drifted into the outskirts of Wiluna, some obtained employment on the sheep and cattle stations while others were content to wander from one group of their kinsfolk to another. Mudjon himself hovered on the fringe of the settlement, ill at ease in the presence of the white men. He obtained food by stealing and by spearing cattle and sheep. As a result he incurred the wrath of the pastoralists and on one occasion he was pursued by a police party which opened fire as he fled over the crest of a sand ridge. Mudjon described this incident in great detail with much gesticulating and a great deal of mirth. He insisted that it was only his ability to hear the bullet coming towards him that enabled him to quickly draw in his abdomen, and escape unharmed.

Gradually he lost his fear of the white man and obtained employment tracking and killing dingoes for which he received payment for the scalps he collected. He subsequently worked on various stations as an 'odd-job man' but never became a stockman like many of his kinsmen. He was unable, or unwilling, to master the art of horse riding.

As he grew older he moved to the outskirts of Wiluna to become deeply involved in upholding the traditions of his people. He was now one of the respected elders, one of the 'law men' and a custodian of the secrets that had come down from the Dreamtime.

This was the man who was to accompany us in our search for Warri and Yatungka, and we were indeed fortunate and privileged to be associated with him during our journey.

Chapter Five

Our plan was to travel north to Glenayle Station to refuel and do a final check of the vehicles. From there we would proceed in a north-north-easterly direction, along the Canning Stock Route for an undetermined distance. Our turning-off point was dependant on receiving an answer to our smoke signals, or, failing this, when Mudjon considered we should turn to the east. We had no specific plans beyond that point. From there our course would depend on the topography and where Mudjon chose to direct us in our search.

Early in the afternoon of 31 July we drove to the Aboriginal Reserve at Wiluna to collect our companion and guide. Mudjon was not in his camp. He was, we were told, 'out bush'. He and the other elders were engaged in 'law business' in the little shed that had been constructed outside the reserve where the sacred objects of the desert people were stored. No uninitiated males and no females might venture near the storehouse. It was the exclusive province of those who had passed through their initiation. A messenger was dispatched to inform Mudjon we had arrived and we waited until the 'law business' had been completed. When he finally appeared he was obviously eager to set forth on his journey.

Quickly collecting a couple of blankets and a piece of canvas from his tent he announced he was ready to depart. With scarcely a glance at his wife or a wave to the others who had gathered around, he climbed into the vehicle and waited impatiently for our party to move off towards his country.

Each vehicle left Wiluna with an enormous payload of fuel and stores. Late in the afternoon we reached a place called Sydney Head, so named because of a resemblance to the entrance to Sydney Harbour. The spot was well known to Mudjon. It was here that his people had gathered after their long walk out of the desert. He pointed out the flat ground where they had danced, the place where the old men had met for discussions on the law. The area on the north side of the Head where they had hunted the kangaroo to supply food for the gathering. As we ate that evening Mudjon spoke again of the events of that time when the elders believed that a better life awaited the Aboriginal people if they moved in from the desert.

We continued on towards Glenayle until a light shining through the mulga scrub ahead indicated that we had reached the end of our day's journey. In a few minutes we were being greeted by Mr and Mrs Ward, whose warm welcome and kind hospitality we had been fortunate enough to experience the previous year.

Glenayle is indeed the 'outpost of civilisation'. Located on the south-eastern corner of the Gibson Desert, one can travel several hundred kilometres to the north and north-east from the station before encountering another white person. It is at the extreme edge of the pastoral country and beyond the station to the north it is impossible for man to eke out a living from the land with his sheep and cattle. Only Aboriginal people can survive in the country beyond Glenayle.

Henry and Mrs Ward established the station shortly after the end of the Second World War. At that time many Aboriginal people were moving in from the desert and Glenayle was often their first point of contact with the white man.

Throughout the years Henry has kept a detailed diary of the daily happenings on the station. He has recorded the names of the desert tribesmen and women as they arrived, he has noted the drovers who brought the great mobs of cattle down the Canning Stock Route and he has written of the trials and tribulations involved in running the station in such a harsh environment.

The Wards have raised a fine family on Glenayle and I admire their courage and their fortitude, and deeply appreciate their hospitality. A drink and a yarn with them after a long desert trip is indeed a pleasure.

The vehicles were given a final check. Everything had to be in first-class order before we could venture into the desert. We would be on our own out there and could not expect help from anyone should we run into difficulties. Glenayle was our last refuelling point and in order to take on as much fuel as possible we jettisoned anything that was not considered an absolute necessity. In the next few weeks we would travel over one and a half thousand kilometres across some of the most difficult country in Australia, and where, at times, the fuel consumption would be down to about one kilometre to the litre.

Water supplies would not present any problems over the first section of our route. We knew that an unlimited amount of good water could be obtained from the springs at Durba Hills, some three hundred kilometres up the Canning Stock Route. Beyond Durba we could not be certain of any further supplies in the desert country we would be traversing.

We left Glenayle with three very overladen vehicles and followed the track to the north-west to halt for the night a kilometre and a half to the east of Weld Spring, Well Nine, on the Canning Stock Route. We chose to make camp away from the well, as the extreme drought conditions had created a dust bowl where the Glenayle cattle watered.

Weld Spring was named after the then Governor of Western Australia by John Forrest who, in 1874, passed through on his historic journey from the Indian Ocean to the Overland Telegraph Line in South Australia. Forrest, later to become Premier of Western Australia and the first Australian-born member of the House of Lords (as Lord Forrest of Bunbury), was leader of an expedition which comprised his brother, Alexander, as second in command, two other white men — James Sweeney and James Kennedy — and two Aborigines — Tommy Windich and Tommy Pierre.

The party discovered the spring on 2 June 1874 and remained there until 20 June. On the afternoon of 13 June they were attacked by a group of from forty to sixty Aborigines who swarmed down from the hill which overlooks the waterhole; they were forced to discharge their firearms to defend themselves and at least two of their attackers were wounded. The Aborigines retreated, and on the following day the Forrest party hastily erected a stone hut near the water to provide some measure of protection from a shower of spears, should they be attacked again. However there were no further signs of hostile Aborigines and the explorers moved away to the east on 20 June. Remains of the 'fort' can still be seen, a reminder to those who now pass that way, of that unfortunate encounter at Weld Spring.

We were interested in locating the site of a corkwood tree that Forrest had blazed on 6 June 1874 with the inscription F/46, denoting that Weld Spring was the expedition's forty-sixth camp since leaving the west coast. The tree was still standing in the mid 1920s and great mystery surrounds its disappearance. Another corkwood which grew at the spring was cut down by an Australian Army party in 1942 on the assumption that it was the Forrest tree. This was placed in the Western Australian Museum in Perth but recent examination of this relic indicates that it was not the tree that the Forrest expedition had blazed. It was, in fact, the work of a later explorer, Frank Hann and the initials J? F that led to the incorrect labelling (these letters were considered by the army officer to mean John Forrest) were those of a person unknown.

Forrest stated in his journal that he marked the tree F/46 and in the early 1900s Frank Hann, who was possibly the first white man to visit Weld Spring after Forrest, states that there were only two corkwood trees in the vicinity of the spring. He noted that one carried Forrest's inscription and he proceeded to mark the other with the letters F. HANN, the mark displayed on the tree in the Western Australian Museum.

Working from photographs of the area taken in the mid 1920s by a dingo trapper which clearly showed the two corkwood trees and the F/46, we were able to pinpoint the position of Forrest's tree and digging revealed the charred roots of a corkwood. The tree had been burnt some time between 1926 and 1942, either accidentally or deliberately, by persons unknown.

A search in the ankle-deep dust around the 'fort' resulted in a most interesting discovery, a spent rifle shell. It was possibly the remains of a Snider bullet. The Forrest party carried Snider rifles and these were the weapons that were most likely used in repelling the attack by Aborigines at the spring a century ago. It is reasonable to assume that the shell was one fired that day, for it was another thirty years before Europeans again visited the locality, by which time the Snider rifle was obsolete.

Chapter Six

From Weld Spring we followed the Canning Stock Route, travelling in a north-north-easterly direction towards the Durba Hills. We were moving in the opposite direction to that taken by the great mobs of cattle that once came down one of the great stock routes of Australia.

Arching across the central desert of Western Australia from Halls Creek in the Kimberley to Wiluna, a distance of about one thousand six hundred kilometres, the Canning Stock Route crosses some of the most inhospitable country in Australia. Belts of mulga trees, great expanses of open spinifex plains and countless sand ridges, all country that the white man feared. It was thought to be waterless country, where only the black man could survive.

What was the purpose of this stock route?

In the early years of this century, the cattlemen in the Kimberley region of Western Australia were seeking markets for their stock, and one such market appeared to be the newly established settlements on the goldfields of Coolgardie, Kalgoorlie and adjacent fields. They requested the government of the day to investigate the possibility of establishing a route from the

Kimberley to the railhead at Wiluna, from which point the cattle could be transported by rail to the Goldfields.

The government agreed to undertake a feasibility study. An expedition would be mounted to examine the country between Wiluna and Halls Creek, and a most remarkable man, Alfred W Canning, was chosen as leader. Born in Melbourne in 1861, he became a surveyor and was appointed surveyor to the Western Australian Government in 1893. During the next few years he carried out surveys in the southern part of the State, as well as being responsible for surveying the rabbit-proof fence which extended from the south to the north-west of Western Australia.

Because of his great experience in his profession and his prowess as a bushman, Canning was the man most suitable to lead a party through largely unknown country in a search of water supplies for travelling stock. Very few white men had previously ventured into the Gibson and Great Sandy Deserts and those that had done so Warburton, Giles, Forrest, Wells and Carnegie, had all suffered great hardships. The lack of water, the intense cold and heat and the interminable sandhills that had been described by those explorers, were challenges that Canning readily accepted.

On the morning of 29 May 1906 he left Wiluna with a party of eight men, twenty-three camels and two ponies. They carried provisions to last several months, well-sinking equipment and water drums with a capacity of one thousand four hundred and fifty-six litres.

Moving slowly from one Aboriginal well to another, seeking assistance in finding water from the Aboriginal people through whose land they travelled, Canning and his men reached Halls Creek on 27 October 1906. Whilst the party recuperated from their ordeal and whilst stores and equipment were assembled for the return journey, Canning submitted a report to the government which indicated that a stock route could be established as an outlet for the Kimberley cattle.

On their long journey south along their outward track the party put down a number of bores, but before they had reached the halfway point a tragedy occurred. One of the white men, Michael Tobin, was speared to death by an Aborigine.

In the vicinity of the waterhole known to the desert people as Waddawalla and later to be the site of Well Forty, Tobin was the first of several white men to die on the Canning Stock Route. He was buried close to where he met his death, near the salt lake that now bears his name. One of the loneliest graves in Australia, it is marked by a marble headstone carried hundreds of kilometres up the Stock Route by camel, and erected over the grave by men who admired the courage of a man who was prepared to face the hazards of the desert country in the early days of the twentieth century. The circumstances surrounding Tobin's death are of considerable interest.

Tobin had, perhaps, the greatest affinity with the Aboriginal people of any member of Canning's party and it is ironical that it was he who died at the hands of an Aborigine. In a way, however, it was Tobin's confidence in his ability to establish rapport with the desert people, his readiness to approach them and to converse with them, that led to his death. As the party neared Waddawalla on their return journey, Canning went on ahead to find a suitable place to camp. Not finding a suitable site near the well he went further afield, finding footprints which indicated there had been an Aboriginal hunting party in the area. Locating a satisfactory camping place near the salt lake, he returned to the well, where he was joined by Michael Tobin and an Aboriginal member of the party, Nipper.

After being shown where they were to camp for the night, Tobin requested the use of Canning's field glasses, as he wished to climb the low hill nearby to ascertain whether any aborigines were in the vicinity. He wanted to talk with any of the local people, as both he and Canning were anxious to locate a waterhole which, they had been told by an Aborigine whilst on the outward journey, was somewhere a little to the east of the lake.

On reaching the crest of the hill Tobin observed a aborigine at the well. He and Nipper returned to where the ponies were standing and, mounting them, rode towards the well. Shortly afterwards Canning heard a rifle shot and he and another member of the party ran towards the top of the hill to investigate. Before reaching it, however, they observed a fully armed Aboriginal man running towards them followed by Tobin on horseback. The Aborigine, on seeing Canning, stopped running and Tobin, dismounting, walked towards him. Canning noted that the aborigine had taken up a stance preparatory to launching a spear, and he shouted to warn Tobin. Despite repeated warnings Tobin continued to advance and Canning, placed as he was about eleven metres from the Aborigine, attempted to divert his attention, but with only momentary success. When Tobin had advanced to twenty or thirty metres he appeared to realise he was in danger. He raised his rifle and fired, at the same instant that the spear was hurled. The aborigine fell to the ground dead, but his spear had struck Tobin in the chest, penetrating several centimetres. The spear was then removed by the victim himself who stated he thought he was 'done for', that he regarded the wound as a mortal one.

On the contrary, Canning did not consider that the injury was so serious and he assisted Tobin to a suitable place for him to lie down. He appeared faint and Canning hurried to meet the camels, which were now approaching, to obtain some whisky. This was administered to the wounded man. He was made as comfortable as possible, but despite the efforts of his companions his condition deteriorated and he died a little after noon on the following day.

Tobin, who was held in high regard by all members of the party, had great confidence in his own ability to communicate with Aboriginal people. After the spearing, he explained to Canning that he had not considered that any aborigine would attempt to harm him. As he approached the Aborigine at the well he noted that he was armed with a spear. He called out, '*Weer colla*' (don't spear). The aborigine turned away only to wheel round and hurl the spear towards Tobin. The missile struck Tobin a glancing blow on the side of the head and pierced his ear. He fired his rifle and pursued his assailant over the hill, where the final confrontation took place.

Why had the Aborigine attempted to kill Tobin at their initial encounter at the well? We will never be in a position to answer this question with any degree of certainty but perhaps this was an action by the aborigine to protect his family, for it was found later that he was accompanied by a young woman and two small children. They were found on the morning that Tobin died crouched under a bush, and disappeared into the desert after the Aborigine had been buried.

After burying their comrade, Canning and his party moved away to the south, to reach Wiluna in July 1907 after an absence of thirteen and a half months. They had proven a stock route could be established across the Gibson and Great Sandy deserts, and as a result of Canning's recommendations the government decided to establish a series of wells along the proposed route. Alfred Canning was again appointed leader with the task of supervising the construction of wells between Wiluna and Halls Creek.

In March 1908 the second expedition left Day Dawn. It consisted of twenty-three white men and one Aborigine, Nipper, the latter having been a member of the original party and a witness to the spearing of Tobin at Waddawalla. Two more white men joined the party shortly after their departure. There were seventy camels and over one hundred tonnes of materials and stores that had to be transported along the route. Included in their goods was the marble headstone destined for Tobin's grave at Well Forty.

Over fifty wells were sunk at an average distance of twenty-seven kilometres apart, a day's walk for the cattle soon to plod down the track from the north.

The tremendous task undertaken by Canning was completed in April 1910 after the first cattle had come down the route. Three small mobs left the Kimberley in 1909, the first being driven by a former Kimberley policeman named Thompson, accompanied by a young Englishman called Shoesmith and two Kimberley Aborigines. The second mob was under the control of Tom Cole, and the third, a Mr Wickham.

Cole, following closely behind the leading mob, became increasingly apprehensive as he observed that Thompson had allowed numbers of Aborigines to travel with him and to camp in close proximity to the droving party. To Cole, with his wide experience of Aboriginal people, there were great dangers in such a close association. His fears were realised when to the north of Well Thirty-seven (known as Libral to the desert people) he noticed some Aborigines wearing clothing he recognised as having belonged to Thompson. These garments could, of course, have been presented to the aborigines, but the finding of Thompson's diary in their possession seemed ominous indeed.

Hurrying ahead of his cattle, Cole discovered the bodies of Thompson and Shoesmith in a shallow grave. They had been speared, presumably by the Aborigines who had been travelling with them as they moved slowly south.

Cole and his party buried the two drovers at Libral Well, which, from that day, became known as the 'haunted well', a place where Aboriginal stockman refused to camp and where white drovers felt uneasy. Cole continued on down the Stock Route with the two mobs of cattle and is credited with having been the first drover to travel the entire route.

Another man to meet his death in the vicinity of the Stock Route was an employee of an oil exploration party, J V M McLennon, who was killed in 1922 with a club by an Aborigine, about fifty kilometres to the east of Libral Well. He too was buried at Well Thirty-seven, the 'haunted well'.

By the end of the 1920s the wells along the Stock Route were badly in need of repair. Some had partly fallen in and much of the wooden structures above the ground had been removed by the desert people for firewood. In 1929, a party under the leadership of a colourful character, William Snell, was sent to recondition the wells between Wiluna and Well Thirty-five. Snell was later to meet a tragic death on the land he took up near the southern end of the Stock Route.

Alfred Canning, then aged sixty-five years, was called out of retirement to complete the task of reconstructing the remaining wells on the route he had established twenty years previously.

Following this, at least one or two mobs of cattle came down almost every winter. For the men who drove them the journey was an arduous one, as it necessitated long hours in the saddle and back-breaking labour when each well was reached. To quench the thirst of the four hundred or more head of cattle that jostled about the water troughs required many hours of drawing water by bucket from the depths of the well and emptying the contents into the troughs. This was done by using a hand windlass, or by a rope passing over a pulley on a whip pole which was pulled by a camel or horse. This was hard work indeed at the end of a long day behind the cattle, but the drovers that came down the Canning Stock Route were a hardy breed: men like Dave Bickley, George Lanagan (whose wife was the first white woman to travel down the route), Ben Taylor, brothers Mal and Len Brown, and the legendary Wally Dowling, to name just a few.

By the 1950s the Canning Stock Route had outlived its usefulness and in 1958 the last mob of cattle came down, driven as far as Well Twenty-two by Len Brown and by George Lanagan for the remainder of the journey.

Today, one of the great stock routes of the world and one that played a fascinating part in the history of Western Australia has been abandoned. Many of the wells have fallen in, the timbers eaten away by termites, the troughs that once catered for the herds of thirsty cattle lie rusting in the desert air. Where once could be heard the noise of milling cattle, the shouting of drovers and the sounds of the desert people as they camped around the wells after the cattle had moved on, today there is silence, broken only by the desert wind as it whistles through the rotting windlasses and whip poles.

The desert people have gone, the drovers have disappeared. Today the only visitors to this fascinating part of Australia are the adventurers in their four-wheel-drive vehicles, who regard a journey along the Canning Stock Route as one of the last great challenges of the Australian outback.

Chapter Seven

We moved north passing wells Ten, Eleven and Twelve and beyond the northernmost boundaries of the pastoral properties. We camped twenty-one kilometres south of Well Thirteen on an open spinifex plain, having crossed sixteen or seventeen sand ridges of moderate height during the day, none of which created any difficulties. Mudjon was pleased to be out in the desert country once more. The section of the Stock Route we were traversing was well known to him. He had passed that way many times before, firstly on foot and, in later years, by motor vehicle. He talked that night of the stars that shone so brightly in the clear desert air, of the names his people had for the most prominent stars, the Milky Way and of some of the myths associated with the heavens.

Making an early start the following morning, we crossed several sand ridges to reach Well Thirteen, a desolate place where time had taken its toll of the work of Canning and Snell. The whip pole had fallen over, the windlass had disappeared and the well itself had collapsed. A few Aboriginal artefacts were scattered around, a reminder that the desert people had once camped there from time to time. But many years had passed since they last sat around their camp fires at Well Thirteen. The Aborigines that once roamed over that country had gone.

Mudjon spoke animatedly of the time, long ago, when he and two companions had walked to the well from Glenayle, a distance of over ninety-six kilometres. He had only been in from the desert for a year or two and felt the need to 'go bush'. The ninety-six kilometres through spinifex and scrub did not trouble a man who had walked hundreds of kilometres during desert journeys in the past. He obtained a great number of spears from the 'spear trees' that grew out to the west, and returned south to the station country with his load of new weapons.

As I sat with Mudjon at the well I thought of the feverish activity there would have been in the past when the thirsty cattle, scenting the water ahead, rushed forward, the stockmen riding hard to hold them back, the bellowing of the animals as they milled about the water trough, the rattling of the pulley in the whip pole as bucket after bucket of water was drawn.

About six kilometres to the north of Well Thirteen Mudjon spotted some 'spear trees' scattered over the spinifex plain. Never able to resist the urge to gather them, he insisted that we stop the vehicles. He strode quickly through the spinifex, barefooted, and seemly unaware of the needle-like clumps. Each tree was examined from all sides for straightness and thickness and, if suitable, was quickly brought down by a few deft blows below ground level with an axe. Not a centimetre of the stem was wasted. Moving rapidly from tree to tree he soon had as many 'spears' as he could carry. These were tied in a bundle and placed on the roof of one of the vehicles. When he had time he would work on them, heating the shafts to facilitate the removal of the bark, and then straightening them by applying pressure with both hands and feet whilst the shafts were supple from the heat.

Mudjon has little or no use for spears as weapons these days but they are tremendously important to him, nevertheless. To

Mudjon uprooting a 'spear' tree.

have spears is, to Mudjon, to have prestige, and to return from a trip into the desert with an enormous bundle strapped to the vehicle elevates him in the eyes of his people.

Having satisfied his urge, for a time Mudjon settled back happily and we resumed our journey. Thirteen kilometres further along the track we encountered the most difficult sand ridge since leaving Weld Spring. The hill was high and the sand extremely dry with no vegetation to give any traction. After several attempts to cross we reduced the air pressure in the tyres, a measure which enabled us to reach the other side with ease.

Three kilometres further on we reached Well Fourteen, situated on a flat between sand ridges. It was a sad sight too, with only the timber trough supports being visible above ground. The well had caved in and no water was available there. A depot had obviously been established there during the construction phase of the Stock Route or during the reconstruction in 1929, as numerous pulleys, steel bars and other pieces of equipment were found nearby. On a white gum tree, growing two hundred and ten paces from the well and bearing one hundred and forty-two degrees, was a blaze indicating that one of the drovers, Ben Taylor, had come down the Stock Route, reaching the well on 2 July 1939.

In the clearing around the blazed tree we found a small fragment of a bottle which once contained a well-known perfume, one that was popular in the 1930s and 1940s. The brand name could still be clearly seen. Who on earth would find the need for a perfume on the Stock Route? Surely not the drovers or the Aboriginal stockmen. Perhaps the bottle belonged to the first woman to travel the route. She accompanied her husband from Bililuna Station to Carnegie Station, with eight hundred head of cattle, a journey that lasted four and a half months.

We reached Well Fifteen shortly after midday. Situated in a white gum and ti-tree flat, it contained potable water and, again, much of the above-ground timber was in very bad condition.

A well on the long-disused Canning Stock Route.

About eighteen kilometres to the north we passed the handcart we had seen the previous year. It was left there some years ago when a party attempting to walk the Stock Route was forced to abandon the little vehicle when the wheels collapsed. Murray Rankin, one of the walkers in that abortive attempt, was determined that he would walk from one end of the Route to the other, and in 1976 he achieved his ambition. Having driven up the Stock Route in a Land Rover and establishing food depots on the way, he, in company with three other bushwalkers: Ralph Barraclough, Kathy Borman and Rex Shaw, left Halls Creek on 12 July 1976. Ralph became ill soon after leaving Bililuna Station and was forced to return while the others pushed on to the south.

Their walk each day usually began about five-thirty a.m. and ended before midday when they reached the next well. They would rest there and move on the following day. In some cases, when they came to their depots, two or three days would be spent before proceeding further along the track. On Saturday 21 August they reached Well Twenty-five and shortly before midday were astounded when two vehicles appeared over the sand ridge just south of the well. We had been camped at Well Twenty-four awaiting fuel supplies, and having found a note at Well Thirty-three on 15 August which indicated that the walkers would probably reach Well Twenty-five on the twenty-first, we drove up to meet them. They were delighted to have company, the first people they had seen for about six weeks. We lunched with them at that desolate spot and took letters and films back for posting when we left, for we would reach civilisation weeks before them. Their estimated date for arrival at the southern end of the Stock Route, Wiluna, was 25 September.

As we continued our journey to the north, the Durba Hills gradually appeared out of the desert plains ahead, with the mesa-type hills of Diebel a few kilometres to the west. We were anxious to reach Durba before nightfall and passing Well Sixteen entered burnt out country completely denuded of all vegetation, and this continued until we reached our destination, the little oasis of Durba Spring.

With its clear running spring water, its huge white gum trees and luxuriant couch grass, it was a popular camping place for drovers in the great days of the Stock Route. They recorded their presence there on the sandstone wall, amongst the paintings left by the Aboriginal people who once frequented the area in considerable numbers.

Because of the supply of permanent water and the pleasant surroundings, Durba Hills was a gathering place for the desert people. The large number of rock paintings and engravings at both Durba Spring and Killigurra Gorge is an indication, not only of its popularity, but of its sacred significance to Aborigines.

In 1906, when Alfred Canning and his small party were camped at Durba Spring, they found a large cache of spears which

Inscriptions of drovers and other adventurers at Durba Hills along the Canning Stock Route. The series of circles at the centre of the photograph are examples of Aboriginal rock art.

they regarded as evidence of an impending attack. Camped on the flat and virtually surrounded by high cliffs affording cover and a perfect launching platform for spears, they were in an extremely vulnerable position and felt justified in confiscating the weapons they had discovered.

Killagurra Gorge, six and a half kilometres north-west of Durba Spring, also contains a spring of fine water. Here, too, are a great number of rock paintings which appear to be more of a secret-sacred nature than those at Durba. Mudjon was very apprehensive at Killagurra and preferred not to enter the gorge proper, yet he was quite content to camp at Durba Spring in close proximity to the paintings there. This was not, of course, his country, and although the area has long been abandoned by the people who once lived there (except for occasional visits by

Aborigines from Jigalong), Mudjon was keenly aware that he was an intruder. He gave the impression that he expected something terrible to happen to him at any moment.

Mudjon and I wandered along the cliff face at Durba as we examined the rock art (*walga*). He indicated various types of edible food as we walked, the fungus (*morabudi*) which is eaten either cooked or raw, the edible berries of the walgoo tree and the flowers of the grevilla (*pandalba*). He told me of the evil man who lives under the surface of Lake Disappointment. A vast expanse of salt about eighty kilometres to the north; the lake is approximately sixty-four kilometres from north to south and forty-eight kilometres from east to west. Perfectly flat except for an occasional island of sand, it receives the water from Savoury Creek, which empties into it from the west.

The evil man, Ngangooloo, remains in his lair beneath the lake's surface during cold or windy weather and ventures forth on calm warm days to roam the land, devouring any Aboriginal people he may encounter. For this reason Lake Disappointment has always been given a wide berth by the desert people.

We had approached the lake from the north the previous year and as we moved closer to it Mudjon became more and more subdued. During the last few kilometres he rarely spoke, and then only in a whisper. We came out on the north-west corner of the lake, the surface of which was dazzling in its brightness as the sun's rays bounced off the brilliantly white salt layer. The small islands far out on the lake had a threatening look about them as they appeared to hover above the surface.

But Mudjon saw none of this. He sat motionless with eyes downcast, refusing to alight from the vehicle. Our suggestion that we should camp under the desert oaks on the lake shore was answered by vigorous shaking of the head. It was no place for a Mandildjara man to spend the night.

Respecting Mudjon's wishes, we moved away from the lake for

Durba Spring.

a distance of a kilometre or two to make camp amongst the
sandhills and desert oaks. It was an eerie place and it was not only
Mudjon who felt uneasy that night. He retired much earlier than
usual but did not follow his normal practice of sleeping close to
the camp fire. Instead, he slipped into the night and rolled his
swag out under the darkest bush he could find. If anybody was to
be devoured that night it would not be Mudjon, but the stupid
white fellows who were readily visible as they slept near the fire.
However the wind moaned through the desert oaks above us and
it was obviously not a suitable night for Ngangooloo to be abroad,
and we were not molested. When Mudjon arrived for breakfast
the next morning, and anticipating some questioning as to why
he had not slept near the fire on such a bitterly cold night, he
announced that he had spent the night some distance away as it
was so hot.

Chapter Eight

Because of the long drought we could not be sure of obtaining further water supplies until we reached Glenayle again, we filled all water containers before leaving Durba Spring. The extent of our search for Warri and Yatungka would depend on the amount of fuel and water we could carry.

We continued our journey north along the Stock Route with one thousand three hundred and nineteen litres of fuel and six hundred and thirty-seven litres of water divided between the three grossly overladen vehicles. It was necessary to exercise extreme caution for broken springs and axles were a real possibility with such enormous loads over the rugged terrain.

Moving slowly, crossing sand ridge after sand ridge, repairing an occasional puncture, we pushed northwards. We waited for Mudjon to indicate when we should leave the Stock Route and enter the trackless desert. Was it possible that the burnt country we had seen the previous year to the east of Midway Well was the work of Warri and Yatungka? 'Might be', said Mudjon, in that non-committal way which can sometimes be so infuriating. Would we examine the area for signs of recent habitation? 'Might be', was again the answer. Should we send up a smoke signal to signal our presence? 'No', said Mudjon. He was quite definite about that.

We could not understand this, for we felt that should Warri be anywhere within a radius of a hundred and sixty kilometres he would see a smoke signal and could reply if he so desired. But for reasons we could never ascertain, Mudjon refused to send up smoke on that day and during the next few days.

As we wound our way slowly along the track Mudjon announced that we would turn to the east at the next well. He had not seen any smoke out in that direction. As far as we knew there was no reason why we should leave the Stock Route at that point, unless it was because we had gone out to the east from that well during our expedition the previous year.

The country around the well, and as far as one could see to the east, was a scene of utter desolation. A fire had passed through some months previously destroying the timber superstructure of the well. The spinifex had disappeared and only blackened skeletons remained of scattered low scrub that once grew there. One plant, however, was growing in profusion, its broad green leaves and stalks standing out vividly against the red soil. This was the native tobacco plant, the *womma*, whose growth had been stimulated by the fire that had scorched the countryside. It had always been highly prized by the desert people and Mudjon gathered it up with great joy, packing it into plastic bags to be smoked and enjoyed at a later time when it had dried. Little did he know that much of the *womma* he collected that day would not be for his own use but would, in the near future, provide great comfort to an old friend.

As we were now moving in an easterly direction and running parallel to the majority of sand ridges we were able to make good progress. Only occasionally was it necessary to cross a sandhill which meandered across our path. There was no indication from Mudjon as to where he expected to find Warri and Yatungka, where he would begin the search, and he still refused to send up smoke.

Gradually a low range of hills appeared above the sand-dunes to the south, the Ngundrayo Hills of the Budidjara. Some years previously, while reading an explorer's journal, I noted that he had visited Ngundrayo in a search for water for his thirsty camels. He had great difficulty in getting his string of camels over the sandhills that surrounded the hills and noted in his journal that they were the worst he had ever encountered.

He found water in the range and in doing so discovered a large number of Aboriginal paintings nearby. To indicate the water supply to others that might pass that way he blazed a tree in the vicinity.

This had captured my imagination and seeing the Ngundrayo Hills from afar during our previous expedition, my companions and I resolved at that time to visit them when we were in the locality again. The task, however, would not be easy. We stood on a low stony rise gazing southwards and it was apparent that a vast ocean of sand ridges separated us from the range. Our maps confirmed this. If it was difficult going for camels how much more difficult would it be for a wheeled vehicle.

Mudjon was eager to go to Ngundrayo. He had wandered through the area long ago but had never reached the permanent waterhole that he believed existed there. It was unlikely that he would find Warri and Yatungka there as it was not Mandildjara country. But if Warri knew that there was permanent water at Ngundrayo perhaps there was a remote possibility that the couple may have moved there if all the waterholes in their own country had dried up.

We cleared a wide area of spinifex and scrub and drove two of the vehicles into the centre of the clearing. We would leave them there, protected from fire, whilst we travelled to the range in the third. Off-loading all but essential supplies, we set off to do battle with the sandhills. We would go as far as possible and should the way be blocked by impassable sandhills we would continue the journey on foot. We were determined to reach Ngundrayo and

In the distance are the Ngundrayo Hills in the Gibson Desert.

explore the range, and locate the rock art described last century by the first white man to visit the area. He remained at Ngundrayo only a day or two, then moved southwards through a gap in the hills without exploring the western half of the range. Perhaps he and his companion were the only white men to have visited Ngundrayo, protected as it was by the vast ocean of sandhills. Who could resist the urge to locate the cave with its paintings; to find the blazed tree and to explore the hills beyond the small section recorded in the explorer's journal?

Our progress was slow as we encountered one sand ridge after another, but the excitement increased as we conquered each one. By late afternoon we found ourselves imprisoned in a network of confused dunes which towered above us on all sides. We decided to camp for the night in a little clump of trees on the basin floor and ponder on our prospects for the morrow.

As the sun sank behind the sandhills I reconnoitred on foot, seeking a passage to the south. I found that it was possible to make a crossing a little to the south-east of our bivouac. Considerable work would be required to level the clumps of spinifex on the approach to the crest, and the track would have to be laid with spinifex and scrub so that maximum traction could be obtained. Having solved the problem of crossing the first sandhill I surveyed those further to the south until darkness forced me to abandon my task. Surrounded as I was by dunes with no landmarks on the skyline, it was necessary to proceed cautiously on my return journey. I did not relish the thought of being lost and spending the night alone without food or warmth. Backtracking carefully, following my outward footsteps, the sight of our camp fire blazing in the basin as I crossed the last ridge was a welcome one indeed. As we sat around the fire that night we talked of our plans for the following day. We felt that we would reach the range by vehicle but, should we encounter any difficulty, we would walk the remaining distance. One thing was certain, we would camp at Ngundrayo the next day.

Getting away to an early start we followed the course I had suggested, crossing the enormous sand ridge at the point I had noted and continuing on over smaller dunes, emerged onto a low gravelly rise. Several small, dry creeks crisscrossed the clearing and there were many artefacts in the vicinity of the rock holes, suggesting this was a favoured Aboriginal camp site in the past, when the water drained off the rise into the creeks.

Ngundrayo now loomed large above the very irregular and confused sandhills, and we pressed on with a sense of urgency and mounting excitement. We broke out of the sandhills onto a claypan with scattered mulga and within a half a kilometre of the range. The country was open, affording comparatively easy going. Our first objective was to locate the cave on the northern face, and we travelled slowly along the foot of the range towards the south-east.

As we rounded a little promontory, white gums were seen at the base of the hill and eager inspection revealed an opening in the rockface. Was this the cave that contained the rock art? Moving slowly inside we could vaguely discern some paintings, but as our eyes became accustomed to the darkness many more could be seen. Surely this was the explorer's cave. But there was no water to be seen and there had been sufficient to slake the thirst of the camels during that first visit. And where were the two large white gums that had been described growing just outside the cave entrance? One fine tree grew a few yards away but where was the other? The tree was inspected and as it showed a small indentation on its north-western side we cleared the bark away, but no inscription could be found. It was most unlikely that this tree had been blazed by white men.

Then, amongst the debris near the cave entrance we discovered the remains of what had once been a large tree. It had fallen down many years previously. The elements and termites had destroyed much of it but the main trunk was still reasonably intact. There was no indication that it had once displayed an inscription. To complete our examination we rolled the trunk over and there it was! The neatly cut opening, without doubt the work of a white man intent on leaving his mark. It was not the work of an Aborigine seeking a carrying dish or spear thrower. The tree had stood for perhaps half a century after the explorers had left, but none who saw it could read its message. Only the desert people had passed that way. The story of the white men with their strange animals would have become a legend amongst the Budidjara and the blazed tree was a reminder of that time. More than three-quarters of a century was to elapse before white men again visited the place, and the tree could not wait that long.

About eighteen metres further along the range to the south-south-east and a little higher, more examples of rock art were found. Further exploration resulted in the discovery of a considerable number of very unusual paintings and engravings, the latter, like most examples of this form of Aboriginal rock art, were of great antiquity, in places being almost completely worn away by the action of wind and rain over the centuries.

On the banks of the small dry watercourse that issued forth from the hill in the vicinity of the cave, were numerous Aboriginal artefacts. Cutting and scraping stone tools and grinding stones used for powdering ochre or perhaps for the more mundane task of crushing seed into flour. During good seasons when water was available in the cave, the area would have been an excellent camping place for the desert people.

We moved to the north-north-west along the foot of the range, and at one and a half kilometres came abreast of native fig trees growing high on the cliff face to the south-east. Nearby was a large cave containing a couple of very interesting elongated stick-figure paintings. A dry creek emerged from the head of the valley to disappear out on the plain. By following up the watercourse it was relatively easy to cross the range and come out amongst the sandhills that stretched for many kilometres to the south.

Returning to the valley we saw evidence of an old Aboriginal encampment on the western side of the creek, and it was here that the explorer had discovered human remains. A skeleton was found, the bleached bones lying under a crude shelter. Were they the remains of an elderly or an invalid Aborigine who had been abandoned by his or her people?

We camped for the night near the entrance, and we proposed a toast to the two men who had visited Ngundrayo more than three-quarters of a century ago. We admired their courage and endurance in travelling through that most difficult and arid country, urging their camels over spinifex plains and sand ridges. It was necessary for them to continually search for water in an almost waterless land while we, latter-day explorers, travelled in relative comfort, with plentiful supplies of food and water. The

The entrance to the explorer's cave at Ngundrayo. Only one white gum is still standing, the remains of the other can be seen lying at the left of the photograph.

cold beer we enjoyed each night after making camp was something that our predecessors could have only dreamed about.

Next morning, after travelling a short distance we drew abreast of a gap in the range. We entered this to find that it opened out into a valley, and it was possible to drive through the hill to emerge amongst the sandhills.

Shortly after entering the valley, Mudjon picked up a small dead branch of a tree and held it aloft. To me there did not appear anything unusual about the object but Mudjon, with his extraordinary vision, had noticed something about it as it lay amongst the spinifex. It had, he said, been cut from the parent tree long ago by an Aborigine, one who had acquired a metal axe from somewhere, possibly from the drovers who came down the Stock Route. Close examination did show small, clean cuts which could not have been made by a stone axe. What I found so remarkable was that Mudjon could notice the marks from a distance of three or more metres. The man never ceased to amaze me with his marvellous powers of observation.

Proceeding along the face of the range we entered another gap, finding a cave in the southern cliff face. This contained several examples of rock art which, being exposed to the full glare of the sun, were very faded. One, however, stood out from the others and was perhaps of more recent origin. It was an elongated figure about two metres in height which stood midway between two piles of stones that had been assembled against the cave wall. By climbing onto one of these it was possible to reach a ledge in the wall where very smooth grinding stones were located. I have no doubt that these were employed in grinding various types of ochre for use in rock paintings. After examination, we replaced them on the ledge, but I fear they will never again be used by the desert people who have disappeared forever from Ngundrayo and from the Budidjara country.

Moving westwards, two more breaks in the range were explored, both of which contained faded paintings. In one, a dry creek meandered across the valley to disappear amongst the spinifex to the north. From the many artefacts found on its banks, it appeared to have been a favourite camping place for generations of Aboriginal people.

We had not discovered any water at Ngundrayo, although Mudjon insisted that there was a permanent waterhole there, his people had often spoken of it. As both water and fuel supplies were low, we resolved to continue our exploration only as far as the western end of the range, and then we would return to our depot away over the sandhills to the north. It was most fortunate that we decided to continue our exploration a little further for a veritable treasure-house of Aboriginal art lay a short distance ahead.

Having reached the end of the range, we noticed white gums growing along the base and observed a number of pigeons flying

Ngundrayo Water.

about. Water must surely be close at hand, and the increasing number of animal tracks converging towards a gap in the hill was a sure indication that a waterhole lay in that direction.

Mudjon, never having visited the Ngundrayo water, had only a vague idea of its location. He now strode briskly forward along the animal pads, confident that this was the permanent water that his people had spoken of so often in the past.

We entered a magnificent gorge of high grass and numerous white gums, and a very excited Mudjon moved rapidly ahead intent on reaching the waterhole as quickly as possible. It was not thirst that was driving him forward, it was because there was water ahead and in an Aborigine who has wandered the desert the urge to see water at every opportunity is something that is deeply ingrained, something that is never lost. Besides he had heard Ngundrayo water mentioned so often that it had seemed like a Garden of Eden to him ,and he had vowed long ago that one day he would see for himself. And this was the day.

As I followed Mudjon I could see a great many rock paintings which were clearly visible on the cliff face on both sides, particularly in those places protected from the direct rays of the sun. A half-kilometre walk along the floor of the gorge brought us to a bifurcation. The animal pads headed into the most easterly branch and when I followed them for a short distance to the head of the gorge I came upon a splendid pool of clear water and an elated Mudjon. The pool was fed by a spring which bubbled out of the ground, a spring of cool, sweet water. There was no doubt about it, said Mudjon, this was the legendary Ngundrayo water of the Budidjara.

He had seen it — and he was happy.

We rested by the water for a time, revelling in the coolness and the lush vegetation around the pool. But we could not long remain in that place, the desire to explore the surroundings was too compelling. Moving along the cliff face I was overwhelmed by

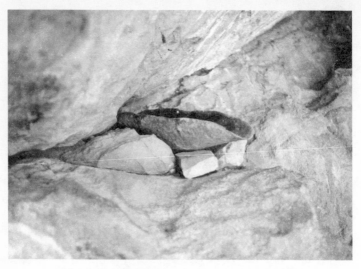

A long-abandoned coolamon, or pitji, at Ngundrayo.

the number of paintings and engravings found in every cave, every indentation on the rock face. Some were visible in almost inaccessible places high on the cliff, some were so bright and vivid that one had the impression they were painted the previous day, that the paint would not be dry; others so faded it was evident they had been untouched for a very long time.

I noticed what appeared to be an old curved piece of wood on a ledge above me, and climbing up to investigate I discovered a wooden carrying dish (*pitji* or *coolamon*) left there long ago by one of the desert people. It contained some old and crumbling vegetable matter, as though the owner had gathered some of the seeds from the grass in the gorge for grinding into flour, had placed the laden dish on the ledge whilst he or she wandered down to the waterhole and never returned. I wondered what could have happened to the owner of that dish. I felt uneasy, as though something terrible had occurred at that place.

It was highly likely that women and uninitiated males were forbidden to enter the gorge because of the large number of paintings and engravings, many of which were probably of a secret–sacred nature. One presumed that the owner of the *pitji* was a woman, for it was woman's work to collect seed. That was not the province of males. Was it possible that a woman had wandered into the gorge, had been discovered and had paid the penalty for her foolishness? Or perhaps the owner had left the dish in the gorge whilst she visited another place. If that was the case why did she fill it with seed before doing so? A *pitji* is a valuable piece of equipment, highly prized by Aboriginal people. It is a food carrier, a water container, it is used for transporting infants. No Aboriginal woman would venture far without one, and would certainly not leave one behind when setting out on a journey. It was interesting to ponder on that mystery at Ngundrayo water.

The southern arm of the gorge did not contain a great amount of rock art. At its head, water was discovered dripping out of the rocks. There was no large pool beneath it, just damp earth and moss.

Retracing our steps we climbed onto the tableland above the pool, and it was obvious that others had been there before us. A large slab of timber had long ago been removed from the trunk of a mulga tree to be made into a spear thrower. A short distance away was a large flat stone which had been placed in an upright position, an Aboriginal direction marker, used as a pointer to indicate water or possibly some sacred object. A few metres further along was a peculiar grinding base plate, with the usual depression in the centre caused by the action of the grinder itself. What was so interesting about that particular plate were the peckings over the surface, the work of humans. What was the purpose of that artistic exercise?

We moved out of the gorge to camp for the night amongst numerous Aboriginal objects and the remains of camp fires of long ago, the site of an old encampment. As we sat round the fire,

Part of the vast gallery of rock art at Ngundrayo.

the excitement of our discovery that day had not waned, it was a once-in-a-lifetime feeling.

I suggested that because the gorge and the pool were of such tremendous significance to the people who once lived in the area and to honour our Aboriginal companion, the gorge should be named Mudjon Gorge and the waterhole be called Ngundrayo Water, the name given to it long ago by the Budidjara.

On present-day maps of Ngundrayo, there is nothing to indicate that once a proud people roamed this country and the names shown are those of white men. And yet every geographical feature was once known to every Budidjara man, woman and child by a particular name.

We sat that night in the place chosen by the desert people for their camp site and used by them for centuries, or even millennia. Gazing at the escarpment silhouetted against the night sky and listening to the sounds of movement in the bush around us, I felt the presence of those who once inhabited the land. We, who had wandered into the area, into a place where few, if any white men had been and where no black man had ventured for many years, felt we were intruders. At any moment a group of Budidjara people would return from the desert and find us occupying their camp site.

Dingoes prowled around the camp during the night and we wondered about the leg of bacon we had left hanging in a bag back at our depot. If the dingoes scented it we would have eggs without bacon for the remainder of the journey and there would be some thirsty dingoes amongst the sandhills.

Next morning, I walked with John Hanrahan into a gorge, adjacent to, and a little south of, Mudjon Gorge. At its head we found a little water and only a few examples of rock art, the artists obviously preferring to display their work on the rock face of Mudjon Gorge.

We climbed to the top of the escarpment to take a round of angles from a promontory near the entrance. We called the place Budidjara Gorge in honour of the desert people in whose country we were trespassing. From our vantage point a vast sea of sand ridges extended in every direction protecting the range and its art treasure from the outside world.

We returned to the vehicle and drove a short way to the south-west to round the end of the range and run towards the south-east, exploring each indentation as we moved. At three kilometres, noting a dry creek lined with gums from a gap in the range and observing animal pads converging on it, we left the vehicle and proceeded on foot.

Moving up the narrow valley we saw rock paintings which increased in number as we progressed. Reaching a bifurcation, we followed the lead to the left a short distance to its head, where water was found dripping down from the rocks above. The lead to the right contained many paintings and engravings and there was a good pool of water at its head. A good pool, but not to be compared with Ngundrayo Water.

We found some extremely interesting engravings in the gorge. On the valley floor was a large boulder with an engraving on one surface. A portion of this was missing, but a search for it in the vicinity was unsuccessful. The surface exposed when the fragment split off showed considerable weathering, an indication of the great age of the form of rock art.

Nearby, another large boulder showed faint peckings, and on close examination I was able to see the outline of a kangaroo. The engraving had been almost eroded, and in that part of the country, where rain falls infrequently, a very long period of time would have been necessary to erase the artist's work.

Apart from the great antiquity of the art on the boulder, what was also of considerable interest was the fact that the rock itself had split into two pieces. This fracture had occurred after the artist had completed his work. For such a large boulder to be fractured, it must have fallen from a considerable height, and yet on examination of the cliff face above there was no evidence to show where it had broken away. I can only assume that, a very long time ago, the engraving had been done high on the cliff and for some reason, perhaps as a result of an earth tremor, it had fallen to the valley floor. The exposed area on the rock face had then been subjected to weathering, possibly for centuries, until it became indistinguishable from the surrounding rock surface.

That particular gorge contained even more examples of Aboriginal rock art than were found in Mudjon Gorge, and I considered an appropriate name for it was Walga Gorge, *walga* meaning painting in the language of the Budidjara.

Chapter Nine

It was now time for us to return to our depot and resume the search for Warri and Yatungka. The couple had not visited Ngundrayo, at least not for some time, despite the fact that it offered an assured water supply even during the prolonged drought that the desert country was experiencing at that time.

Perhaps they were not aware of its existence, but this would be highly unlikely as Mudjon, Warri's hunting companion of the past, knew that it was there, and in all probability they had spoken of it as they moved across the plains together. Perhaps Warri and Yatungka had found permanent water in their own country, and would only move into Budidjara territory as a last resort. It was not their land.

The return to the depot was far less difficult than the outward journey, armed as we were with the knowledge of every sandhill crossing. We arrived back at our starting point to find our provisions, including the leg of bacon, intact. Although only seventy-two hours had elapsed since we left to visit Ngundrayo, it seemed much longer than that. It had been a most rewarding and an exciting time. Not only had we located the cave and the blazed tree which had been the purpose of our journey, but we had also discovered an enormous art gallery.

Leaving our depot we followed our tracks to the point where we had turned south towards Ngundrayo. There I took a round of angles to fix the position and facilitate the progress of any party (hopefully, in the first instance, one from the Aboriginal Sites Department of the Western Australian Museum) attempting to reach Ngundrayo and who would, presumably, wish to travel the route we had mapped.

It is to be hoped that the rock art of the Budidjara at Ngundrayo will be studied and recorded before the four-wheeled tourists descend upon the place in large numbers, removing artefacts and leaving that pathetic form of rock art, their initials, amongst the work of the desert artists. Ngundrayo, at present, is exactly as it was when the Budidjara people moved away for the last time. It has not been desecrated in any way, the high sandhills that surround it have protected it from the white man and it has kept its secrets.

We, having made such an exciting discovery, had a duty to report our findings to the Aboriginal Sites Department. This was done on my return to Perth, but a detailed study of Ngundrayo cannot, unfortunately, be carried out for some time. The staff of the Department must give top priority to recording details of Aboriginal sites threatened by the great number of mining ventures in Western Australia. Those sites that are not in immediate danger must wait. This is only right and, as Ngundrayo sleeps amongst its encircling sandhills and does not appear to be of interest to geologists and prospectors, it has a low priority.

However, to protect it, I have used the Aboriginal names for the topographical features during this narrative, names that will not be found on any map. I hope that they will be incorporated into maps in the future for they honour the people of the desert who once lived there. If not, then the white man's nomenclature will remain, giving no indication that Aboriginal people once inhabited the area and used names that had come down to them from the Dreamtime.

Mudjon indicated that we should continue towards the east, to the low hills known to him as Moongooloo. We had been there during a previous expedition, but on that occasion we did not find water. Mudjon, however, was adamant that there was a permanent waterhole there. He knew this, he said, because although Moongooloo was in Budidjara country, he visited the place many times with the Mandildjara when they had been walkabout.

We reached our old camp site on the south-western side of the hill, a rather desolate spot. Apart from a few scrubby trees and an occasional clump of spinifex there was no vegetation. There were no animal tracks to be seen, no sign of bird life, and obviously there was no water in the vicinity.

We climbed the rocky slope to the tableland and obtained an excellent view of the country we had traversed, as well as the land we were about to enter in our search. Ngundrayo was visible as a dark blue line on the horizon, protruding above the rich red colour of the intervening sandhills. There was no sign of smoke in any direction. If Warri and Yatungka were still alive out in the desert, they were not advertising their presence.

Returning to the vehicles we drove through a narrow gap which opened out into a large basin, approximately one and a half kilometres wide and surrounded by hills on all sides except to the north-east. We had gone into this valley during the previous year and, to indicate the narrow entrance, had blazed C/76 on a bloodwood tree. At that time we were retracing the route taken by the Honourable David Carnegie, hence the letter C.

On that occasion we were greatly excited because we found the basin to be a little oasis. Although no surface water was found, I have no doubt that water could be obtained by digging, and that

reach Moongooloo water in the morning by walking through one of the gaps in the range.

From our camp on the edge of a dry creek two gaps were visible, one subtending one hundred and sixty-seven degrees and the other two hundred and thirty-three degrees. Next morning

Mudjon straightening a spear shaft after heating it in a fire. Note the sand in his hands to insulate them from the heat of the shaft.

Mudjon chose to enter the latter, following up the creek that issued from it. Outside the entrance there was a great deal of evidence that it had been a popular camping place for the Aboriginal people. Numerous stones and cutting instruments lay about, and here and there collections of stones of the quandong fruit where feasting had taken place in the past.

On entering the gorge we climbed gradually in a south-westerly direction, following the animal pads in the valley floor. The cliff face on either side was extremely rocky and varied from eighteen to twenty-four and a half metres in height. Many caves in the face were explored, some found to have a few examples of rock art but there was nowhere near the number and variety of the paintings seen at Ngundrayo, nor were there any examples of engraving seen.

A half a kilometre from the entrance to the gorge we reached a shallow waterhole, about fifteen and a quarter metres long by two

A close-up of the sharp stone used by Mudjon to scrape the bark off the spear shaft.

and a half metres wide, and about sixty-four metres further on came to a magnificent pool, twelve metres by four and a half metres and at least three to three and a half metres deep.

Mudjon was elated. This was the waterhole he had spoken of so often during the last few days, the waterhole he had visited long ago. It was only because of his insistence that we had ventured to this part of Moongooloo. There were many paintings nearby, and Mudjon pointed to one close to the cliff top which, he said, indicated the path to the tableland above, which the Budidjara used when moving to the south and west.

We retraced our steps down the gorge, finding a wooden scoop near the creek, as well as a great number of stone cutting knives on the site of the old camp. There were also many grinders, some intact, some broken into many fragments.

Mudjon was anxious to begin work on the spears he had collected as he wished to return to Wiluna with a large number of weapons. After lighting a fire he proceeded to work the shafts slowly through the flames, withdrawing them from time to time and applying pressure to the heated sections to straighten them. He did this by using his foot as a lever and his hands to apply counter pressure. So that his hands were not burnt he scooped sand into them for insulation before gripping the heated wood. Having satisfied himself that the spears were as straight as possible, he then peeled the bark away. The heat had lifted this in many places and it could readily be removed. The shafts were then scraped laboriously with a knife to remove any irregularities on the surface. In the past this was done with a sharp stone scraper, but Mudjon was quite happy to abandon the traditional method for a white man's knife, in view of the great number of sticks that awaited processing.

I again walked up to Moongooloo Pool, this time in the company of John Hanrahan, and climbed the ancient path to the plateau above. Our purpose was to explore the second gorge, the entrance of which was readily visible from our camp. We were disappointed, however, for no rock art was found, nor were any artefacts seen during the long hot walk. Although we followed the gorge right to its head not a drop of water existed there.

After passing through the entrance and onto the plain, we again found evidence of many old camp sites, in one of which the remains of a digging stick was found. Could this — or the wooden scoop found earlier on in the day — have been left at Moongooloo by Warri and Yatungka? No, said Mudjon. He was certain that the couple had not been to the place in recent years. The scoop, he thought, had been left by the Aboriginal family we had encountered the previous year, and the digging stick had been abandoned by the Budidjara people when they left the area for the last time.

Chapter Ten

Having located Moongooloo waterhole and ascertained that Warri and Yatungka had not been there in recent times we decided to make a flying visit to the north for thirty to fifty kilometres. It was in that direction that we had sighted burnt country as we travelled westwards the previous year, and we considered that a search should be made of that area before proceeding further to the east.

We again established a depot, leaving two of the vehicles and most of our provisions and fuel there, taking one vehicle and supplies for two or three days and sufficient fuel to travel two hundred and fifty kilometres. Although the sand ridges extended to the horizon to the north, we could avoid many by running parallel to them in a west-north-west direction for several kilometres until we broke out into salt flat country.

We camped for the night in some low scrub between sand ridges. Mudjon was in high spirits as he spoke of the two men of the Dreamtime, the Wati Kudjarra, and told some of the legends of his people. He was immensely proud of the fact that he had been able to locate Moongooloo waterhole when we had expressed some doubts as to its existence.

It seemed strange to me that he had not spoken of Warri and Yatungka since we had left Wiluna, except in reply to direct questioning. They were the reason he had brought us into the desert, yet he avoided making any reference to them.

He still showed no inclination to send up smoke, yet on our expedition the previous year he had fired the spinifex at every opportunity in the hope that Warri would reply. To us it seemed obvious that before venturing in any particular direction we should send up a signal and search the horizon. If there was no answer then perhaps we should look elsewhere, but Mudjon displayed no enthusiasm for that line of reasoning.

We steered north-west for nineteen kilometres to emerge onto a large salt flat. Turning north we ran for another nineteen kilometres over rough open country, then passed through low scrub to come out onto a circular saltpan. The surface was soft, the vehicle tending to break through the salt crust, and there were some anxious moments before we finally reached hard ground on the other side. To be bogged to the axles in a salt lake in that isolated country was not a pleasant thought.

As we drove off the salt surface Mudjon drew our attention to a shining object at the end of a low promontory which stretched out into the lake. Something was reflecting the sun's rays and Mudjon suggested that it 'might be' a tin can or a bottle, at what he referred to as a 'white fella's camp'. I doubted whether many 'white fellas' had camped in that desolate part of the country, and the treeless and windswept tongue of land reaching into the lake would be the last place I would choose for a camp site.

Not wishing to take the vehicle out onto the lake again, we walked across to the headland, the salt crackling under our feet. The 'white fella's camp' turned out to be a piece of mica, there being a considerable quantity of this material lying about. Mudjon was greatly amused by the whole incident. The joke was on him and he enjoyed it immensely.

We ran on to the north-east for another five or six kilometres to a low hill that was just visible above the sandhills. We climbed to its highest point where I took a round of angles.

The country to the north-west was open with few sandhills evident, whilst to the east and south-east the red crests of sand ridges stretched like an ocean to the horizon, a forbidding sight. The low range on which I stood was capped with quartzite and devoid of any vegetation. It disappeared beneath the very high sandhills at intervals, to appear again sixty to one hundred metres away and continued in that fashion for eight or nine kilometres. From my vantage point there was no sign of any waterhole, and there would have been little to attract the Aboriginal people to the area in the past.

A small claypan was visible a short distance away to the south-east and we drove across to investigate. It was very shallow and had not contained water for a very long time. A search around the edge resulted in the discovery of a couple of grinding stones. This had been just a short-term camp, used by the desert people as they travelled through their country after rains, when a little water could be obtained from the pan.

We steered south-south-east to a long hill that rose abruptly out of the sandhills and made camp at the north-eastern edge. I climbed to the top to take a round of angles whilst my companions walked around the base to ascertain whether a waterhole existed and whether there was any evidence of recent Aboriginal habitation.

I sat high above the plain watching the late afternoon sun casting shadows across the low sandstone range to the north. Far away to the east the pink sandstone of a conical hill was picked out by the last of the sun's rays, against the blue-grey colour of the low-lying country around it.

Allowing my imagination full rein I could almost see the string of camels of the exploration party that passed that way more than three-quarters of a century ago. They came in across the desert from the north-north-east to make camp a little to the north of my observation point, and the following day moved away to the south, anxious to leave that waterless stretch of land behind.

My companions did not find water during their walk, nor did they find any evidence of Aboriginal habitation in the past. No artefacts, no rock art and it seemed the hill was avoided by the people of the desert for some reason. Mudjon could not enlighten us concerning this as he had not been into the area previously. He could only shrug his shoulders when questioned.

We decided not to search any further to the north. We would return to our depot at Moongooloo the next day and from that point move out to the east.

Before sunrise on the following morning, Mudjon, who never failed to scan the sky each day when he rose from his bed, noticed a haze far away on the horizon to the north. To us it was nothing, but to Mudjon it was smoke, the work of the 'Fitzroy Crossing mob'. Fitzroy Crossing was several hundred kilometres away but Mudjon was certain that a group of Aboriginal people from the settlement were on walkabout and had fired the country the previous day and their smoke was now visible.

On other occasions he had indicated that a haze was caused by the 'Warburton mob' (the Aboriginal community near the Warburton Ranges, far to the east) or the 'Jigalong mob' to the west. It was only with the aid of field glasses that we could discern what Mudjon could readily detect with the naked eye.

We returned along the outward track for several kilometres, then turned to the north-west towards a long low hill which stood out in the early morning sunlight. The urge to explore this was irresistible after our discoveries at Moongooloo. Eleven kilometres across open country brought us to a high sand ridge which barred our progress. Between us and our destination were many enormous sandhills and it was clearly impossible to proceed in that direction.

'Ripple' stone on top of a plateau in the Western Gibson Desert.

We veered to the north-east onto more open country for a distance then turned to the west to run in between the ridges. Several breaks were visible in the escarpment, indicating that watercourses probably issued out of the hill. We explored one of these, walking up a gorge for a kilometre to its head and a very large rock hole. It would hold a very large volume of water after rains fell but it was completely dry, giving some indication of the severity of the drought that gripped the desert.

We walked across the high plateau to the western edge of the hill and gazed down on the salt flats that extended away to the west. I was interested to see large slabs of ripple sandstone on the plateau — evidence that the area had been submerged long ago.

At the north-eastern end was a most impressive sight, a sheer drop of over sixty metres to the plain. There was little animal or bird life seen and I doubt whether there is any permanent water in the area. No rock art adorned the hillsides and it appeared that the hill, Wannoo, as it was called, was not popular with the Aboriginal people. Mudjon stated that Wannoo was avoided by the desert people, they were afraid of it, but I could not discover the reason for that fear. Perhaps it was because of its proximity to the salt flat country to the west, country that had always been given a wide berth in the past.

We did not explore the southern portion of Wannoo, for we wished to reach the depot at Moongooloo before nightfall. However, despite all our efforts, we were forced to make camp for the night sixteen kilometres short of our destination, reaching the depot early the following morning.

As soon as we arrived, Mudjon began working on his spears, anointing the shafts with cooking oil which, he said, made them easier to straighten at a later date. Having completed that task he decided to go walking and I accompanied him in the hope of learning a little more about the ways of his people.

He missed nothing as he strode barefoot through the spinifex, pointing to 'pussycat' tracks here, goanna (*baanga*, sometimes mispronounced bungarra by white people) holes there, a snake track around a clump of spinifex, the tracks of four camels. These animals, he said, had been running at high speed. He suggested that they had been surprised by the noise of our vehicles when we entered the valley on the first occasion. How did he arrive at that conclusion? Shrugging his shoulders to indicate that the reasons were obvious to anyone, he pointed out that the tracks were several days old and made about the time of our arrival. The animals had been moving away from our point of entry and they were moving very quickly. A camel would not run at that speed unless it was frightened and the noise of our vehicles would be strange and terrifying to the animals in that part of the country. It was as simple as that!

Mudjon searched for bardi grubs (*loongee*) in the root systems of the stunted shrubs but without success. He blamed the long drought for the absence of that great delicacy. In good seasons he would obtain his fill in a short time but for the moment they were gone, 'all finished'.

We walked to a low stony ridge to survey the land to the east and south-east, country over which we would be travelling during the next few days. Mudjon gazed eastwards for a long time without speaking.

He was, he later said, thinking of the time, long ago, when he and others of the Mandildjara roamed their country, the western boundary being visible from our observation point.

He spoke of the waterholes to the east: Ngeega, Pidjirri, Ngowell, Malliadoo, where he had often camped with his people. This was, he said, his last visit to his own country and he wished to see for the last time the watering places around which the lives of the Mandildjara once revolved.

He had returned to search for Warri and Yatungka, the last of the people in the desert. If they were found alive he hoped they would be willing to join their kinsfolk in Wiluna. Then there would be no reason for him to visit his homeland again. It was very sad for him to move through the land where once his people hunted and laughed and sang around the camp fires. All that remained to show for several thousand years of occupation were a few artefacts around the old camp sites. He wanted to see as many of his old haunts as possible on this journey for his heart was 'too sad' for him to come again. Unless of course he could gather together a group of his people who would be willing to move back to their country. This would make him glad and he would die a happy man in the land that had been given to the Mandildjara in the Dreamtime.

During our walk back to the camp Mudjon was silent. The reminiscences of the morning had produced in him a profound sadness. He had no desire to continue working on his spears and lay down, deep in thought, in the shade of a tree. He was deeply disturbed at what had happened to his people and to their culture and social organisation. To look out on the land of his boyhood wanderings, now a vast empty desert, was extremely depressing to Mudjon.

Later, when he was more communicative, I spoke to him about suitable names for the two gorges we had explored in the range. The waterhole he said, had always been known to the desert people as Moongooloo Kapi, but the gorges themselves had not been named, the whole area being called Moongooloo. The hills were referred to by the general name of Yapo Boolee (Stony Hill). It was the waterhole that was important, not the range itself or any gorges and valley it contained, unless they contained permanent water. It would be most appropriate if we named the gorge after two of the Budidjara people. Could Mudjon suggest two names? There were, he said, two men of the Budidjara who had impressed him long ago when he came to Moongooloo, Dabbalya and Yowyungoo. It seemed appropriate that their names should be preserved for posterity on maps of the Western Gibson Desert so that future generations looking at such maps would know that Aboriginal people once lived there. The main gorge containing Moongooloo Pool (or Kapi) should be called Dabbalya Gorge and the lesser one, Yowyungoo Gorge, after the two men of the Budidjara.

Late in the afternoon Mudjon returned to his spear making, heating and straightening, barking and scraping until he had a large number of completed weapons. These were tied together in a bundle and strapped on top of one of the vehicles ready for an early start the next day. We would leave Moongooloo and move further into the desert, steering east for the low hills of Kata Kata about ninety or a hundred kilometres away over the sandhills.

Chapter Eleven

We moved out of Moongooloo, travelling in a general south-easterly direction for eight kilometres, then taking a more easterly course to run between the sand ridges. By midmorning we had reached a low gravelly rise on which grew a few scattered mulga trees, the whole area crisscrossed by dry, shallow watercourses.

The place was well known to Mudjon. It was Birrill waterhole where, long ago, he had challenged the fleeing Warri to return with him to Mandildjara country and face the judgement of the people for his wrongdoing. There was not a drop of water in the well, not even the slightest moisture to indicate that some could be obtained by digging. There was no evidence that Warri and Yatungka had been to Birrill in recent times.

Mudjon indicated the spot where he had stood when the spears thrown by Warri and the angry men of the Budidjara had rained down near him. He located the place where as a young man on a visit to Birrill, he had eaten the fruit of the quandong tree, the seeds he had discarded being readily found by scraping away the surface soil. He showed us the place where the Budidjara liked to camp when they came to the waterhole, where the soil was soft and easy to fashion into a comfortable sleeping place. Nearby were a number of artefacts, including a portion of shield, perhaps broken in a fight long ago. From the top of the rise there was nothing but sandhills and low scrub to be seen to the north, the east and the south. Away to the west Moongooloo was still visible above the crests of the sand ridges.

Continuing in an east-south-easterly direction we passed the rock hole known as Barragoodingo. Mudjon was navigating from one waterhole to another without the aid of any features on the landscape. There were no hills, no tall trees, nothing to help him to orientate himself, yet we were travelling in trackless country from one point to another as though they were joined by a highway. Mudjon did not consider there was anything unusual about it. He had, he said, walked the country many times in the past and to him there was no difficulty in navigating without the aid of landmarks or a compass.

We camped that night in a little clump of mulga amongst the sandhills. Despite the fact that we had travelled for ten hours that day we had covered less than sixty-five kilometres, such was the difficult nature of the country we were traversing. It was fortunate that we ran parallel to the majority of sand ridges and it was rarely necessary to make a crossing. Mudjon was very quiet as we sat around the fire and, thinking he was not well, I inquired after his health. He was not ill he said. He was deeply concerned for the safety of Warri and Yatungka. He feared they might be dead. He could, 'feel it in my heart'. On that depressing note we turned in for the night.

Moving off the next morning to the east-south-east we found it was necessary to cross several sandhills that meandered across our path. At twenty-six kilometres we came out onto a low stony ridge which afforded us a view of the surrounding countryside. An unnamed reddish escarpment was visible a few kilometres to the south across a shallow valley. At least it was not named on our charts but I am sure that the desert people referred to it by name. I regret that I did not question Mudjon about it at the time for it was close to Mandildjara country and would have been known to him

We broke out of sandhill country and now travelled over open spinifex plain for ten kilometres. At that point Mudjon suggested that we take a more southerly course. There was a rock hole in that direction. Warri, he said, knew its location and we should visit the place to see whether there were signs of recent habitation.

Two and a half kilometres' travel brought us onto burnt country and to Mudjon there was no doubt that it was the work of Warri. The firing had been done in strips, it was the work of man and there were no human beings in the area except Warri and Yatungka. But they had passed that way a long time previously, a year or perhaps even longer.

Five kilometres further on we crossed another burnt strip and shortly afterwards reached an open gravelly area, the site of Ngoongoo rock hole. Some moisture was noted in the bottom of the well but despite energetic digging by John Hanrahan nothing more than a little, slightly damp soil could be found.

Mudjon was now certain that Warri and Yatungka had been alive a year or so previously. They had camped at Ngoongoo while water could still be obtained by digging and, whilst there, they had moved about the country in the vicinity, hunting and food gathering. The burnt patches were evidence of that activity. When water became too difficult to obtain they moved away and Mudjon suggested that they would have gone towards the east.

As it was very late in the afternoon when we reached Ngoongoo we suggested that we make camp there but Mudjon was unwilling to do so. He was anxious to reach another waterhole which was 'close up', and where he felt he might locate Warri and Yatungka.

Bowing to his wishes, we went eastwards, but the 'close up' was further off than we estimated. After travelling six and a half kilometres we again encountered burnt country, and as it was almost dark we again suggested that we make camp. Mudjon was

Windbreaks and the remains of fires near Walloogoobal.

very keen to press on, he wanted desperately to reach the waterhole. We reluctantly continued, for travelling at night in that type of country is fraught with danger, with a very high risk of staking a tyre.

After crawling slowly along for another three kilometres, winding through mulga scrub, we considered the risks too great to proceed further and stopped for the night. We had gone nine and a half kilometres since leaving Ngoongoo and had still not reached the 'close up' waterhole. However Mudjon insisted that it was very near to our camp and he would go there on foot next morning.

We had travelled less than fifty kilometres since our last camp, for the country was very difficult to traverse — dotted with sandhills interspersed with very dense thickets. The scrub had taken its toll and as we had several punctures during the course of the day.

After dinner I took out my diary of the previous year and found that the bearing I had taken of the smoke we had sighted out to the east on that occasion ran very close to our position. We did not know what distance we were from the smoke at that time but considered it was from ninety-five to one hundred and sixty kilometres away. Consequently, it was likely that Warri and Yatungka were firing the country within a few kilometres of the spot we had elected to make camp. Mudjon noted that the country had been burnt about a year previously, but it appeared that Warri and Yatungka had not returned to the area since that time.

Our departure was delayed the next day as the Land Rover's radiator had been perforated, presumably during our passage through the scrub in the darkness, and repairs were necessary before we could proceed. Whilst these were being done, Mudjon walked out to the waterhole, hoping for some sign that Warri and Yatungka had been there. He found evidence of fairly recent habitation but the couple had moved on when the water supply was exhausted.

On his return he set about firing the spinifex, sending up smoke signals, the first time he had done so during the journey. He now thought that Warri and Yatungka may have gone to a waterhole called Millen to the south-west, and said he hoped to make contact by smoke. However there was no reply, either from Millen or from any other direction. The signal rose high into the sky then moved horizontally, an intense grey pall spreading over a wide area. It would have been visible for one hundred and thirty to one hundred and sixty kilometres, but Warri had not seen it or had chosen to ignore it. Or, what was now a possibility in view of the dry waterhole nearby, he was no longer alive to see it.

We travelled less than a kilometre over a series of low gravelly rises to reach the rock hole known as Walloogoobal. It was, as Mudjon said, 'close up' to our camp, but a long way from Ngoongoo.

Situated in the bed of a dry and rocky creek it, like all the waterholes we had visited recently, was quite dry. There was no

The first sighting of footprints near Walloogoobal.

doubt that Warri and Yatungka had camped for a considerable time in the vicinity. They had dug into the earth to obtain sufficient water for their needs, and a broken wooden scoop near the well was, perhaps, some indication of their desperate efforts to survive at Walloogoobal.

Nearby were the ashes of several camp fires, an abandoned digging stick, an old rusty tin containing many holes and a discarded hair belt, normally used by Aboriginal men for carrying lizards and other small game. The remains of a dingo were scattered about, and Mudjon suggested that Warri and Yatungka may have been forced to kill one of their beloved animals for food, something that an Aborigine would do only as a last resort. A dry waterhole does not hold any attraction for birds and animals and any game would move away or perish, leaving little for an elderly Aboriginal couple to live on.

Mudjon led us to the north over a stony rise to what had been a favoured camping place for his people in the past. There were several windbreaks there which had been constructed by Warri and Yatungka using branches and spinifex, and the ashes of several fires were nearby. These were 'cold time' camps, said Mudjon, which had been abandoned when the water supply was exhausted.

It was here that we noticed footprints for the first time and Mudjon immediately identified them as having been made by Warri and Yatungka. We followed them for several hundred metres across a rise to the sandhills. Mudjon indicated that they were 'both weak fellas', and the dogs that accompanied them were also in very poor condition.

We returned to Walloogoobal where John Hanrahan climbed into the depths of the well and threw out a large quantity of dirt and shale, but his efforts were fruitless. It was a long time since there had been water available at this well.

About twenty-seven metres to the west was an odd little grey-white rock firmly embedded in the gravelly soil. At its base

The 'Warrida Stone' near Walloogoobal.

were some strange scratch marks on the ground which were quite fresh. These puzzled us until we realised that Mudjon had gone off in that direction while we were working at the well and we suggested that he was responsible. I questioned him about the significance of the stone to the Mandildjara people, for I felt certain that such an object would have meant something to the desert people.

At first he dismissed the subject, stating, with a shrug of his shoulders, that it was 'nothing'. Later he told me the stone had been put there by 'early time people' but he had no idea of its purpose. He did not admit to being responsible for the scratch marks, but information he later gave me concerning that stone and other similar stones we encountered led us to believe he engaged in some ritual at Walloogoobal.

The stones were the work of a man from the Dreamtime, Warrida, and they denoted his camp sites as he moved across the country on a journey from the Bindibu country on the Western Australian–Northern Territory border, to the place where he died, about one hundred and sixty kilometres south of Walloogoobal. Warrida was a 'good fella' and the stones were left to indicate that water could be obtained nearby. Perhaps Mudjon believed that by scratching the ground adjacent to the stone, water would come to Walloogoobal or to any other waterhole where Warri and Yatungka might be camped. In any case Mudjon would not admit having indulged in any such action.

Warri and Yatungka had gone in a northerly direction when they retreated from the dry well of Walloogoobal and we followed their tracks towards the low hills, visible to the north. At nine kilometres the country became very rough and we were forced to abandon the vehicles and go on foot across stony hills to the rock hole known as Baabool to the Mandildjara.

Baabool, too, was bone dry. Warri and Yatungka had dug deep into the earth in their attempt to reach water, but without success. The bundle of dry spinifex that lay near the well was evidence of their failure. When water is carried for any distance in a *coolamon* or *pitji*, to prevent spillage from the motion of walking, Aboriginal people placed spinifex in the dish, breaking the flow of water and preventing loss of precious fluid. Yatungka had brought a little bundle of the grass to Baabool, anticipating that she would obtain sufficient water to enable her and Warri to proceed to the next waterhole. When nothing was found, she had tossed the grass aside, possibly with disgust and rage, and the couple moved on, without water and without knowing where they would find an assured supply. That, at least, was Mudjon's interpretation of the events that had taken place at Baabool.

Where had they gone in their now desperate search for water? The rocky nature of the country prevented us from tracking them, but Mudjon was certain they would have made for a waterhole a little further to the north. We placed tremendous faith in Mudjon. Not only was he familiar with the land, his own country, and knew every waterhole, but he was able to put himself in Warri's position, to think as Warri would have thought when in that situation. He would go north from Baabool and there was no doubt in his mind that Warri would have gone in the same direction, heading for Kata Kata.

We swung away to the west to avoid the hilly country and emerged onto an open plain which extended to the north as far as the horizon, a vast flat land uninterrupted by even the smallest hill. It was excellent country for firing and Mudjon busied himself igniting the tall spinifex that lined the banks of a shallow creek which rose in the hills to the south-east and spent itself out on the plain.

We moved on to the north of the Kata Kata hills and climbed to the highest point to survey the countryside. If Warri and Yatungka were alive, said Mudjon, they must see the smoke which had by then risen to a height of five hundred to a thousand metres and, flattening out, had spread horizontally for many kilometres. From our observation post we searched the horizon in every direction, paying particular attention to the north and north-east, but there was no answer. The sky remained clear.

Mudjon remained to search the horizon while the rest of the party moved out onto the plain to fire the spinifex and scrub that lined a creek. I felt that if Warri and Yatungka had not seen our previous signal it was a pointless exercise to send up further smoke, but it was Mudjon's wish and we acceded to it.

The grass was tinder dry and flared up immediately on being touched with a torch, sending up a cloud of bluish-white smoke. Where the scrub grew amongst the spinifex it, too, ignited with the intense heat, the green leaves and branches burned furiously, throwing up columns of black smoke. Whilst we were engaged in the task I was interested to note that as soon as we commenced the operation, several hawks appeared overhead, wheeling and diving through the smoke, searching for any small game that might be flushed out by the flames. We had not seen any bird life for some days and yet they appeared the instant the first smoke spiralled into the sky.

Mudjon remained on the hill, silhouetted against the sky of late afternoon, watching for some sign that his old friend was still alive out there in the desert. It was almost dark before he could bring himself to abandon his post. He came down the northern face of Kata Kata, igniting the grass as he moved, and as we sat around our camp fire that night the heights above us were dotted with dozens of small fires as though scores of Aboriginal families were camped on the hillside, as though the country had come alive again and the Mandildjara people had returned home.

Mudjon was very depressed. The signals we had sent up on three occasions that day had gone unanswered, signals that would have been visible for a hundred and sixty kilometres in every direction. Warri and Yatungka must have seen them — if they were alive. They had not replied and the conclusion to be drawn was that they had not survived, that their search for water after leaving Baabool had been unsuccessful.

I thought it would be ironical if, after many thousand years of roaming the Western Gibson Desert, the last of the nomadic Aborigines there had succumbed, not from old age or disease but from their inability to find sufficient water to survive. For several millennia the country had satisfied the needs of the desert people and it seemed that the last of them, the couple who had chosen to remain there, had perished because there was not enough water to keep just two people alive. The land too, was dead, the result of the greatest drought this century, and possibly for centuries. We had arrived too late, said Mudjon, perhaps two or three weeks too late.

Chapter Twelve

There was an air of despondency as we discussed the situation at our camp below Kata Kata, and Mudjon was of the opinion that it was pointless to continue the search for Warri and Yatungka. There had been no replies to the signals we had sent and there could only be one reason for their failure to acknowledge them, they were dead. He knew, he said, for he could 'feel it in my heart'.

Mudjon suggested that we should visit another waterhole the next morning. It was situated less than a mile away to the north and we wondered why, if it was so close to our camp, we had not continued on and camped there. He offered no plausible reason for this, but I believe he was reluctant to proceed to the well that afternoon because he felt sure we would find the bodies of Warri and Yatungka in the vicinity of the waterhole. It was as though he wished to delay the discovery as long as possible.

I was restless that night, waking several times, unable to settle into a deep sleep. The prospect of a gruesome find within the next few hours disturbed me. Mudjon, who lay one or two metres away was also restless, tossing from one side to the other, and I had no doubt he was troubled for the same reason.

Lying on my bunk shortly before dawn, staring up at the incredibly clear sky, I had a strange feeling I was being watched by somebody or something. I sat up and gazed about but could see nothing in the darkness. I remained sitting for a long time and as the light increased I was startled to see two eyes watching me from where our camp fire had been. Initially I could not discern what creature was behind the eyes but after a time a shape became visible. That of a wild dingo, crouching in the warm ashes of our fire. I could not believe that one of the wariest and most intelligent animals in the Australian bush would venture so close to human beings.

I softly called to Mudjon, and as I did so the animal struggled to its feet and staggered slowly away into the surrounding bush. It was terribly emaciated, a further indication of the toll the long drought had taken on the desert inhabitants.

When Mudjon stirred I spoke to him of the amazing sight I had just witnessed. He was not surprised, for he was already aware of the animal's presence. It had come into the camp during the night and after eating some scraps of food had moved to Mudjon's bunk and attempted to get under the blankets. He had sent it away on several occasions and it had finally desisted in its efforts to share Mudjon's bed and had curled up on the site of our fire, attempting to extract a little warmth from the ashes that remained. Despite the fact that I had slept little during the night, I was unaware of Mudjon's actions at the time and none of my companions had heard anything unusual.

The dog, explained Mudjon, was one that belonged to Warri and Yatungka and had been abandoned by them. I found this difficult to understand because Aboriginal people are devoted to their animals, and it may be recalled that Warri had once refused to leave the desert when he found he would have to leave his beloved dogs behind. Even if the animal had been abandoned I felt that it would have followed as long as it had the strength to walk. I believe that Mudjon did not really consider that the dog had been discarded but that there was something far more ominous about its presence in our camp. I, like Mudjon, was now convinced that Warri and Yatungka were dead, that they had perished somewhere in the vicinity and their sole surviving dog had remained nearby, too weak to travel further in its search for food and water.

When we had arrived the previous evening it had been attracted by the scent of the water we carried, and after observing us from the safety of the surrounding bush it had staggered into the camp after we had retired for the night. It was interesting that it had only attempted to obtain warmth from Mudjon's bunk. It was unafraid of him despite the fact that he had sent it away several times, yet my soft call to Mudjon caused it to move away into the bush. The dog was a friend of the Aborigine but not of the white man.

We watched for any further signs of the dog as we breakfasted but it did not appear again. We left food and water for it for we were sure it would return as soon as we had left the area. Unless it found further supplies of water it would perish within a few days and we had not seen water since leaving Moongooloo.

We moved towards the waterhole that Mudjon had spoken about. We were apprehensive as we approached the belt of mulga surrounding the well, convinced that somewhere amongst the trees we would find the bodies of the last nomads of the Western Gibson Desert.

As we moved into the flat stony clearing around the well we saw two crude shelters amongst the trees, one seventy metres and the other ninety metres to the north-west. We fully expected to find the bodies of Warri and Yatungka there and as we approached, Mudjon quickly moved away into the scrub to the west as though unwilling to be the first one to make the discovery.

There was a tremendous feeling of relief to find nothing in

either shelter and we shouted the good news to Mudjon, who then hurried across to inspect the camps. Near one we found an old and rusty meat loaf tin which had been opened, not by the usual method, but by a knife which had been thrust into the can in several places until a hole had been made large enough to allow the contents to be extracted. Several years ago a small party had visited Warri and Yatungka and had left them a supply of tinned food, and that rusty can was almost certainly part of the gift. It had not been opened by a white man but by one who either did not possess a can-opener or who was ignorant of its use.

The well was one and a half or two metres deep, with an opening ninety centimetres by one metre and, as expected, it was quite dry. The sides had been plastered with spinifex to prevent them from collapsing, and nearby was a bundle of bracken which at one time had been used as a well cover to prevent animals from fouling the water supply, and to reduce evaporation.

A few centimetres from the mouth of the well were the ashes of a small fire. It is possible that when Warri and Yatungka were forced to leave Baabool without having obtained water there, they arrived at the well and finding that it, too, was dry, began to dig desperately, for if they could not find water there they would perish. When darkness came they continued digging by the light of a fire which had been lit as close as possible to the well to provide some illumination. They had eventually obtained some water and had remained at the place for some time, camping under the shelters they had erected until the supply was exhausted and it was necessary for them to gather their possessions together and move on once more.

Chapter Thirteen

In which direction had Warri and Yatungka gone when they could no longer obtain water at Kata Kata? There were waterholes out to the north-east, said Mudjon, but if Ngoongoo and Walloogoobal and Baabool and Kata Kata were dry then the other wells would also be dry. In the olden days when his people roamed the desert, we asked, there must surely have been a waterhole where, during severe drought, they gathered and were able to survive until the rains came. There was one such well, said Mudjon, which the old men of the Mandildjara had said would always contain water, even during the longest drought, and in difficult times the desert people would converge on the soak they knew as Ngarinarri.

Did Mudjon think that water would still be available at Ngarinarri? Would Warri and Yatungka attempt to reach it after leaving Kata Kata?

In the days when Aboriginal people wandered the desert, said Mudjon, there were men who possessed special powers and who could ensure that water would flow into the wells so that the men, women and children would not perish, so that the Mandildjara tribe would not disappear from the earth. The old people had said that there would always be water at Ngarinarri, but they spoke of other times. There were no men in the desert now with the special powers needed to bring water to the wells and it was possible that Ngarinarri, too, was dry.

Warri knew of Ngarinarri, he had camped there many times in the past with his people. But it was a long way off, a great many sandhills must be crossed before it could be reached, and Mudjon felt that Warri and Yatungka were in such a weakened state when they left Kata Kata that it would be impossible for them to walk to Ngarinarri.

Mudjon was reluctant to continue the search. He had expected to find the bodies of Warri and Yatungka at Kata Kata well and had been greatly relieved when no such discovery was made. But he was convinced they were dead and he did not wish to stumble across their bodies amongst the sandhills.

We felt, however, that we must at least attempt to reach Ngarinarri. If the couple had struggled there and were still alive we would offer any assistance we could. If they had perished there, then we would know the fate of the last nomadic Aborigines in Mandildjara country. Should we fail to find them at Ngarinarri we would return to civilisation knowing that somewhere out amongst the sandhills towards Ngarinarri were the remains of the last of the desert people.

The absence of any replies to our smoke signals had convinced Mudjon that to go to Ngarinarri would be a waste of time, but we argued that it was possible that Warri and Yatungka had seen our signals but were too weak to answer. We could not abandon our search at this stage but must proceed towards Ngarinarri with all possible speed.

We had little fuel in reserve for such a journey, the vehicles, during the heavy going of the previous two weeks, had consumed a greater quantity than we had anticipated, but we were unanimous in our desire to reach Ngarinarri. Once again we would establish a

Man-made shelter near Kata Kata well.

depot and run out in one relatively unladen vehicle with sufficient provisions and fuel for three or four days.

We studied our map of the area in great detail to plan the quickest and the easiest route to Ngarinarri. The well, of course, was not marked but Mudjon was able to indicate its approximate position, roughly north-north-east from our depot. In a direct line the country appeared impassable, with one parallel sand ridge after another, and it was obvious we would have to detour to the east. Mudjon volunteered the information that in the old days when the Aboriginal people moved between Kata Kata and Ngarinarri they would follow a chain of waterholes, swinging in a wide arc to avoid the worst of the sandhill country. On his advice we would proceed east-north-east to clear the sand ridges then turn to the north for several kilometres and finally swing round to the north-north-west to run into Ngarinarri.

Soon after leaving the depot we crossed an area of burnt

country and Mudjon again found the footprints of Warri and Yatungka. They were moving towards the east-north-east, heading towards the waterhole that existed out in that direction.

Nine and a half kilometres further on we came to a well known as Ngargin, located amongst some rather pathetic looking mulga trees. Several small windbreaks had been erected in the vicinity, suggesting that Warri and Yatungka had been able to obtain a little water and had remained there until the well was dry.

We continued to the east-north-east for another twenty-one kilometres to the well of Wangabaddi. Mudjon was our navigator, we relied on his knowledge of the country to guide us. He was leading us from one waterhole to another through almost featureless country, without tracks to guide him or a compass to assist him. He shrugged his shoulders, as was his fashion, when we commented on his skill, saying it 'was nothing', that he was following the 'main road'. By this he meant we were travelling the same paths that his people had trodden for centuries as they moved between the wells. But one associates a main road with a broad track of cleared country along which vehicles of all descriptions can travel, while the 'road' we moved along was unmarked by a single vehicle. There was not even the faintest suggestion of a footpath to indicate that the desert people once moved to and fro across the land.

Wangabaddi soak was located in the centre of a flat stony clearing about a hundred metres in diameter. A few spindly mulga trees struggled to survive in the rocky ground, although on the northern edge of the clearing grew a little clump of healthier looking specimens.

The well was three and a half metres deep, and it would have been an extremely difficult and even dangerous undertaking to climb into, and out of, the shaft, especially if one was in a weakened condition. The well was dry and not even the slightest moisture could be found after extensive digging.

Warri and Yatungka had camped at Wangabaddi on many occasions in the past. The remains of many fires and several windbreaks were discovered, and at one of their old camp sites was a spear, a digging stick, several old cans and a grinding stone. What was of special interest was something wrapped in a piece of ancient canvas wedged in the fork of a mulga tree about forty-six metres from the well. Mudjon appeared not to notice the object and made no comment although I was certain his keen eyes would have seen it long before we did. We were fascinated by it but as Mudjon was acting in a peculiar manner we did not wish to investigate immediately for fear of offending him.

Our first thought was that either Warri or Yatungka had died and the remains had been placed in the tree, and Mudjon's actions reinforced that assumption. We waited until he had moved off to the north, past the clump of mulga and out onto the sandy spinifex plain to search for footprints before we attempted to examine it.

John Hanrahan climbed the tree and passed the bundle down for inspection. The covering was a piece of tattered canvas, possibly the remains of a groundsheet that Warri had been given long ago. It was unfolded carefully and with some trepidation, and the contents were found to be not human remains as we expected, but the bones of an animal! What on earth was the reason for wrapping animal bones in canvas and placing them high in a mulga tree at Wangabaddi? Was it possible that one of the Aboriginal couple's dogs had died and they had given it a tree burial? Closer examination showed the remains to be those of a kangaroo, but the mystery remained.

When Mudjon returned from his excursion out on the plain the bundle had been replaced in position in the tree and once more he made no reference to it, passing close by without a glance towards it. Anxious to hear his explanation I mentioned our discovery to him. His eyes remained on the ground, indicating that he was fully aware of its presence and that he was a little afraid of it.

We did not inform him that we had taken it down and had some knowledge of the contents because, again, we did not wish to offend him. He offered no suggestion as to what the bundle might contain but in response to my question as to whether it might be 'secret business' he replied, 'Might be', and did not wish to talk about the matter any further.

Ninety metres south of the well was a semicircle composed of five stones of the same type of greyish-white quartz we had seen at Walloogoobal. They were firmly set into the ground and a distance of six metres separated the two ends of the arrangement. These, too, were the work of Warrida of the Dreamtime. He had found water at Wangabaddi, he had camped there and had left the mysterious stones to indicate he had passed that way.

A little further to the south was a small cleared area with several artefacts on the periphery. The place, said Mudjon, was a little dancing ground where formerly his people, when camped at the well, would dance and follow a path that wound past the stones of Warrida towards the waterhole.

On leaving Wangabaddi we continued in an easterly direction towards the sandhills to the north, and after travelling twenty-four kilometres a remarkable little hill capped with yellow-pink sandstone was visible a little to the south-east. Although it was off the 'main road' it had often been visited by the Mandildjara in the past, for near its base was a rock hole, and the waterhole and hill were together known as Birri Birri.

Here, at Mudjon's request, we halted in a clearing for he wished to fire some high spinifex and scrub which grew in a shallow depression running across the open space. The tinder-dry grass burned with an intense heat, igniting the green scrub and sending enormous columns of black smoke skywards.

From the top of the vehicle we looked towards Ngarinarri,

Windbreak near Ngargin well.

about thirty kilometres distant, but the sky remained clear. Mudjon did not appear at all surprised for, he said, Warri and Yatungka had not replied to our earlier signals and he did not expect an answer on that occasion. They did not send up smoke because they could not and he again indicated that they were dead.

We pushed on towards Ngarinarri and after going six and a half kilometres further to the east, we rounded the eastern extremity of the sandhills and turned to the north-east. There were sandhills still to be crossed before we could reach the well but they were no longer an obstacle to our progress.

In the cabin of the vehicle it was hot and noisy as we ground along for another nine and a half kilometres. There was little talk, for all of us had been affected by Mudjon's profound depression: we wanted desperately to get to Ngarinarri but feared what we might discover there. It was late afternoon and we knew we could not reach the well that day and we were pleased, for it would be better to approach it in the morning rather than stumble onto it in the darkness.

The vehicle heaved itself up a low sand ridge and as we reached the crest Mudjon, who had been sitting quietly beside me, apparently uninterested in the world about him, suddenly shouted and pointed excitedly towards the north. There was smoke out there, he said, he was sure he had seen smoke. We peered in the direction he indicated and there it was, a faint wisp of smoke spiralling into the blue-grey sky of that late hour of the day.

There were great cries of joy from all members of the party. There was somebody alive out there, somebody had survived the long walk to Ngarinarri. Was it Warri or was it Yatungka or were, by some miracle, both of them alive? Mudjon was overjoyed that at least one of his people would be found alive after having convinced himself that his old friends had perished.

I took a fix on the smoke and found it bore two degrees from north, and on looking at the map I found that the spot that Mudjon had indicated previously as being Ngarinarri's position, was within half a degree of that bearing.

We wanted to press on with all speed to reach the well but it was an impossible task and darkness forced us to make camp in a valley between sand ridges where there was a little wood for our fire. On top of the ridge to the north grew a large and rather gnarled tree and Mudjon, who was now in a euphoric mood, said that it had been growing for a very long time. He had seen it many times before on his journeys between Ngarinarri and Wangabaddi and the old people had told him it had always been there, that it had been planted there in the Dreamtime.

As we sat round our camp fire that night, Mudjon spoke animatedly of the times that he had roamed the desert with Warri, where they had hunted and what they had hunted. He was obviously tremendously relieved by the sighting a few hours previously and he talked about his people far into the night.

We were all excited at the prospect of finding the Aboriginal couple alive, but at the same time I had a strange feeling of uneasiness, perhaps it was sadness. I could not help thinking that that night would be the last that Warri and Yatungka (presuming both were alive) would spend alone in the desert together if they chose to return to Wiluna with us. The long years they had spent together without the company of other human beings, wandering their ancestral land, might come to an end within a few short hours. We were about to intrude into the lives of the last nomadic people in the Western Gibson Desert, and in doing so it was possible that we might be responsible for bringing to an end a way of life that had gone on for several thousand years.

Ever since Wati Kudjarra had moved through the land creating the features on the landscape, there had been Aboriginal people in the desert. If tomorrow Warri and Yatungka decided to leave with us then, for the first time since the Dreamtime, there would not be a single Aborigine in the country of the Mandildjara or, indeed, in the whole of the Western Gibson Desert. That was a sobering thought, one that weighed heavily on me and one that greatly disturbed my sleep that night.

I wondered why our smoke signals, which certainly had been seen, had not been answered earlier. Was it possible that Warri and Yatungka did not wish to leave their country and had no desire to make contact with us? Our progress across the land could be gauged by our signals and it would be apparent to them that we were moving along the 'main road' between waterholes, and that somebody was leading a party towards them, and who else but Mudjon would be guiding such a party? At his last meeting with Warri, Mudjon had told his friend that one day he would return to lead them out of the desert, that with advancing age they could not remain alone in their country. Was it possible that Warri and Yatungka feared Mudjon's return and refrained from sending up smoke to indicate their position? But surely they must be in dire straits if the country we had passed through in the preceding two weeks was any indication, there being little game of any kind, and not one of the waterholes we had encountered in well over a hundred kilometres of travel had contained a drop of water. Mudjon believed they must be in very poor physical condition and would be prepared to leave the desert, at least until the rains came and the long drought ended.

Perhaps Warri and Yatungka were determined to spend their last days in their own country rather than be removed to a strange and, to them, frightening way of life. Was there a change of heart at the last minute and a decision made to acknowledge our last signal when they realised we were heading towards Ngarinarri and would find them even if they did not send smoke?

We had no wish to disturb them or to interfere with their way of life and should they desire to remain in their homeland and were in reasonable physical condition we would leave provisions with them and on our return to Wiluna would arrange for contact to be made at intervals to offer any assistance they required. However if they were weak and ill and wished to remain, could we just drive away and leave them, knowing they would surely die without adequate food and without medical attention? We sincerely hoped that such a situation would not present itself.

On the other hand, if they chose to go out with us, we would be haunted by the knowledge that we had removed the last of the nomads from the desert.

Those were the thoughts that weighed so heavily on me that night near Ngarinarri.

Chapter Fourteen

We rose early, for we were eager to make contact with the man or woman who had signalled us. Travelling almost due north on the bearing we had obtained the previous evening, we had gone eight kilometres when Mudjon called a halt and proceeded to fire the spinifex once more. Almost immediately an answering smoke rose on a bearing of thirty-five degrees and we changed direction towards it. Two and a half kilometres on, our new course brought us to the crest of a long sand ridge which ran roughly east-west to the horizon and there, on the wide open plain between the sandhills, were flames and smoke rising from a long trail of burning spinifex.

From our observation point there was a distance of one kilometre to a sand ridge to the north, the intervening flat country being covered with spinifex and occasional low scrub. Almost due north of our position and about four hundred metres distant, another sand ridge, which had its origins away to the east, terminated on the plain. With binoculars I searched the plain for a human being amongst the burning spinifex, but without success. It was obvious that somebody was moving out there, for at intervals there would be a sudden burst of flame as a new patch of grass was ignited. A long trail of smoke rose slowly in the still air of the morning and a blackened strip of burnt country denoted the burner's progress across the plain.

Then I saw the figure, moving slowly eastwards, unaware of our presence on the sand ridge to the south. We were disturbed that only one person was visible. Was it Warri or was it Yatungka? A highly excited Mudjon said that, without doubt it was Warri. We searched the plain and the sandhills beyond with our glasses but there was no sign of Yatungka. Had she perished, leaving Warri alone in the desert? Mudjon did not know but he intended to answer that question as soon as possible. He could contain himself no longer and plunging down the northern face of the sand ridge he strode briskly out to intercept Warri, who still continued moving eastwards, intently firing the country, still not aware that he was being observed.

As Mudjon walked rapidly through the spinifex he, too, fired the grass to attract attention, but Warri continued on to the east. It was not until Mudjon was within one hundred metres that Warri caught sight of him. During the time that Mudjon had been seeking to intercept him, Warri had moved off the flat country onto the southern side of the sand ridge which terminated on the plain, and it was from that elevated position that he first became aware of Mudjon's presence.

Through my glasses I saw Warri stop abruptly to stare at Mudjon, then move down off the sand ridge towards him. The two old friends met, but there was no demonstration of joy, no handshakes, no clasping of one to the other. Instead they faced each other from a distance of six metres for at least half a minute, each apparently making a quick appraisal of the other. Presumably some words were then spoken, the gap between the two men closed, and immediately they began to walk back towards our position.

There was still no sign of Yatungka, and Warri did not appear to be looking for her as he followed Mudjon through the clumps

Mudjon's 'smoke' which drew a response from the desert to the north.

of spinifex. It was indeed strange that the two nomads had not been walking together that morning and I feared the worst.

On reaching the base of the sand ridge on which we stood, Warri halted whilst Mudjon continued up the incline to our position. Where was Yatungka? Was she still alive? we hurriedly asked. To our immense relief Mudjon explained that she was indeed alive and was, at that moment, gathering food out to the east where the quandong trees grew and would return to Ngarinarri later in the day.

Warri remained standing at the base of the dune while we talked to Mudjon. He was in an emaciated condition but despite his poor physical state there was a dignity about the man that impressed me immensely. He watched us intently but showed no desire to move closer, and it was not until Mudjon spoke to him again that he came nearer, accepting a drink which we offered. He drank slowly, savouring every mouthful, for he had carried no water with him when he left Ngarinarri that morning and since that time he had walked over five kilometres.

Warri was naked and was not wearing the string belt that Aboriginal people normally wear when hunting, and it may be recalled that a belt was found discarded at Walloogoobal. He carried one non-barbed spear, about two metres in length, and a spear thrower, but his morning's hunting activities had not met with any success, for he carried no game with him. The fire stick that he had used to fire the country had apparently been abandoned out on the plain when he encountered Mudjon. If there were any dogs with him when he left Ngarinarri that morning they were nowhere to be seen, possibly they had picked up our scent and had disappeared into the sandhills to the north before we could see them.

Warri was about one and a half metres in height, extremely thin, with the skin hanging in folds at his buttocks. His hair and wispy beard were matted and, lodged above his right ear, was a wad of chewing 'tobacco', a well-masticated mixture of a plant and the ash of the mulga tree. Several depressions were noted on his forehead and I thought these were probably due to a disease which erodes the skull. Both his eyes were markedly inflamed, the right causing considerable discomfort, necessitating frequent rubbing with a hand for relief. His right eyelid drooped slightly and he appeared to be suffering from trachoma, which, being in an advanced stage, would greatly reduce his level of vision.

There was a swelling on his chest close to the midline and his rib cage could be clearly seen, so wasted was his body. Numerous scratches and scars were visible over his trunk, possibly due to frequent falls in his weakened state, or from burns sustained during sleep near the camp fires.

On his left arm a fragment of an old blanket had been used as a crude form of bandage, but there was no wound or infection apparent. His arm, however, showed considerable wasting, it was weaker than the right and I assumed that the cloth had been wrapped around the limb in the belief that it would strengthen the arm in some way.

His right leg was also wrapped in a piece of cloth, covering an infected lesion which appeared to cause considerable pain, for Warri took his weight off the leg at every opportunity by leaning on his spear.

Mudjon explained that Warri and Yatungka had seen our smoke the previous evening and had decided that Warri would go out in that direction to see who was approaching Ngarinarri, while Yatungka would walk to the quandong trees to gather the fruit which had been their main food in recent weeks.

Early that morning they had gone their separate ways, Yatungka to the east while Warri moved in a more southerly direction, eager to discover who had been signalling him and fearing that he might be passed by. For that reason, he had been firing the country as he walked, anxious to send up as much smoke as possible to indicate his position, for he was not sure that his smoke the previous evening had been detected. As he was not engaged in hunting activities he had no need of his dogs that morning, so they had accompanied Yatungka on her journey to the quandong trees.

We intended to drive to the camp at Ngarinarri to await Yatungka's return, but we had great difficulty in getting Warri into the vehicle. He was terrified, he trembled and appeared to have no concept of how to climb into the cabin, making many feeble attempts but always stepping down again. It was only with a great deal of encouragement and soothing talk from Mudjon that we were finally able to get him into the cabin, and I am sure he would have run away into the bush if it had not been for his faith in Mudjon.

As we started the motor and moved off down the northern face of the sand ridge, Warri became even more terrified than before, burying his head into Mudjon's chest and perspiring profusely. The roar of the engine as we churned up and down the sand ridges on the way to Ngarinarri was almost more than the desert man could bear and Mudjon kept up a patter of talk to reassure his old friend that no harm would come to him.

At five kilometres we passed through some mulga trees into low scattered scrub and halted beside a small clearing, the camp of the desert people, their home of recent weeks. There was little to indicate that two people had spent much of their time here as they attempted to sit out the drought. A low windbreak, the ashes of several fires, two spears and their worldly possessions lying in the red soil of the camp. A wooden carrying dish containing a small steel axe head with a crude handle of mulga wood, a small piece of old canvas, a few battered tins which had been treasured and carried from one camp to another, and a small shovel without a handle.

Those few possessions, with the addition of the spear and spear thrower that Warri carried and perhaps a digging stick and carrying dish that Yatungka had taken with her, were all they had to assist them in their fight for survival at Ngarinarri. There was no food of any description in the camp and no water in any of the receptacles. It was a day-to-day existence, collecting enough water from the well and gathering whatever food that could be procured each day to keep them alive, and judging from Warri's appearance they were fighting a losing battle.

Ninety metres north of the camp the scrub gave way to a claypan, approximately three hundred and sixty-five metres from east to west and one hundred and forty metres wide. A low sand ridge rose up just beyond it to the north and two low rises were visible about three kilometres off, one bearing fourteen degrees, the other three hundred and forty-seven degrees.

Sixty-eight metres out on the claypan was the well, Ngarinarri, which had sustained the desert couple; the well the old men of the

The great moment: burning spinifex and a lone figure on the plain.

Mandildjara said would never run dry. Near the opening some green herbage grew and I noted a crudely fashioned wooden carrying dish close by, which, said Mudjon, was for the use of the dogs, being filled with water scraped from the bottom of the well by Yatungka.

The entrance to the waterhole was almost a metre in diameter, leading into a shaft which rapidly narrowed until at the bottom, three and a half metres down, it was little more than thirty centimetres across. We found we were unable to reach the bottom and could not determine whether water was available there. Because our own water supply was low we considered replenishing it from the well if the water was drinkable and if Warri and Yatungka decided that they would have no further use for it.

We returned to the camp and shortly afterwards Yatungka came through the bushes towards us. She was accompanied by several dingoes which stopped when they scented us then crept away into the scrub. Yatungka showed no sign of any emotion, she did not speak to Warri to question him about the strangers, showed no recognition of Mudjon and gave the impression that visitors to the camp were an everyday happening.

She was younger than Warri and, like him, was without clothing but, although emaciated, she appeared to be in much better physical condition. She was about one hundred and sixty-five centimetres in height and balanced a large wooden dish full of ripe quandongs on her head. On reaching the camp she placed the container on the ground in front of Warri who immediately began to eat the fruit as though he had not tasted food for several days.

We selected a place to camp a little to the north of where Warri and Yatungka had chosen to live, between them and the claypan. We shared our meal with the nomads, who greatly appreciated the tea, damper, tinned meat and jam that we supplied. After living almost exclusively on quandongs in recent times such variety and quantity of food was overwhelming.

Mudjon sat with them as they ate, engaging them in conversation for, like us, he was anxious to learn how they had fared during the long drought, and they in turn sought information of their sons and kinsfolk in Wiluna.

After they had eaten their fill we asked Yatungka if she would collect some water from the well and she readily agreed to our request. Where we had great difficulty in getting down the shaft and were unsuccessful in reaching the bottom, Yatungka descended with ease. She used a small can to scrape up the water, ladling it into a bucket which we had lowered on a length of rope, but it was readily apparent that we would not be replenishing our water supplies at Ngarinarri, for the liquid that Yatungka obtained was a yellow-brown colour and the flow into the soak was very slow indeed. Twenty minutes of hard work produced less than four litres of rather putrid water, and this was poured into the wooden dish on the surface for the dogs.

A delighted Mudjon with Warri.

It was Yatungka who had managed to obtain sufficient water to keep herself and Warri alive, and it was she, too, who had been able to walk long distances to collect food to sustain them. Warri was unable to do those things and he was kept alive only by the industry and skill of the woman that he had 'wrongfully' taken as his wife those long years ago. Without Yatungka's devotion, Warri must surely have perished long before our encounter with them. He was utterly dependent on her for survival.

I wondered what Yatungka would have done if Warri had died at Ngarinarri. Would she have attempted to walk out of the desert? She would have been unable to carry sufficient water for such a journey, the nearest water supply to the south was well over one hundred and fifty kilometres away. Without food and water and in her weakened state she could not have gone half that distance. I believe that Yatungka would not have left Ngarinarri, that she would have remained there, alone in the desert until she, too, perished. It was unlikely that, having spent most of her life wandering with her husband, suffering great hardship and adversity, she would leave him after his death. She would remain with him, but without the will to live she would not survive long.

After dinner that night we walked to their camp, anxious to hear their story; how they survived, details of their retreat to Ngarinarri and whether they intended to stay in the desert or go south with us. Mudjon, who was still euphoric about finding them both alive, plied them with questions.

When their sons and other kinsfolk had moved out, leaving them alone in the desert, the seasons were good and they had been able to wander the Mandildjara country obtaining sufficient food and water as they moved. They would remain in the vicinity of a waterhole, building a windbreak for protection from the biting winds of the desert winter or placing brush in a suitable tree to shade them from the sun during the summer, and move out into the surrounding country gathering food, firing the

Warri with his spear and spear thrower. Note how the spear thrower is being used to take weight from his infected leg.

country and hunting the game. Warri would carry one or two spears and a spear thrower while Yatungka took her digging stick, a wooden scoop and a carrying dish. They would return to their camp late in the day to sit around the fire and eat the food that had been collected during the day's foraging.

It was not necessary to go hunting every day and during the times they remained in camp Warri would work on his weapons, repairing old ones and making new ones. When they tired of one place, or when food became too difficult to obtain, they would gather a few basic necessities together — spears, spear thrower, dishes, tins, a knife and axe — and move off to the next waterhole. Surplus spears and grinding stones were left behind, for they reduced mobility. They would be used again when the wanderers returned in a month or a year.

Moving along the path trodden by countless generations of their people they would ignite the country at intervals, their passage being marked by long narrow strips of burnt land. Firing had a threefold purpose in traditional Aboriginal life. It flushed out any game that may have been sheltering in the clumps of spinifex, it indicated to others their progress across the desert and it regenerated the earth and stimulated the growth of plant life, so that within a short period green shoots would appear in the blackened soil to attract the animals to be hunted by the people who burnt the land.

Aboriginal people practiced what has become known as 'fire stick farming' and it was a custom which assisted nature in maintaining vegetable and animal life in the desert. In areas that have been abandoned, where burning of the country is no longer carried out, where the waterholes are not kept open by digging and clearing, animal and bird life has largely disappeared. They, over the centuries, had, to some extent, become dependent on the Aboriginal inhabitants for their existence, and in vast areas of the desert, where formerly there were wells and soaks to provide

With the exception of some spears, these were the worldly possessions of Warri and Yatungka. The fruit has been collected from the quandong, or Walgoo, trees.

water, there are now only depressions in the soil to indicate where once animals, birds and humans gathered to drink. Without the Aborigines to maintain the watering places the desert game was forced to move to more hospitable regions.

Warri and Yatungka, of course, did not fire the country to signal their movements, for there were none of their people left to read the signs, but whether hunting or just moving from one place to another they still burnt the land, it was natural for them to do so, it had always been done by their people and it was through force of habit that they ignited grass and scrub.

On reaching a waterhole they would spend days or weeks there before moving on, either because the game was depleted or they felt the need for a change. In that way they would travel to the boundaries of their country and then return along their outward track. A particular waterhole may not be visited more than once or twice a year and the duration of stay depended on the availability of water and food or just the urge to move on.

In recent years, however, the long drought had produced an alteration in their normal pattern of progress across the land. They were forced to move more frequently than before, for not only was the water supply limited but food was no longer readily available.

In their final retreat they remained at each well until the water was exhausted and then struggled on to the next, fearing that they would be too ill and weak to reach Ngarinarri. They also feared that even if they managed to get there the supply might fail, leaving them marooned in the desert.

Mudjon asked whether they intended to remain at Ngarinarri or whether they would go with us. They would, they said, accompany us on our long journey south. They had reached the end of the road, they were weak and there was nowhere for them to go from Ngarinarri. They could no longer live in their own country without the help and support of the young people and there were none left in the land of the Mandildjara.

Warri and Yatungka wanted to see their sons again, but they wondered what kind of welcome would be extended to them by others who knew of their transgression of the law. Mudjon, as an elder of the Mandildjara, and one with great authority amongst the Aboriginal people, assured them that no harm would befall them when they reached Wiluna. He had discussed the matter many times with the other elders and it had been agreed that no penalty would be exacted, no punishment inflicted and that the wrong doing of long ago would be forgotten.

After we returned to our camp that night the dingoes, which had been skulking somewhere out in the darkness, quietly moved in to join Warri and Yatungka around the camp fire. They remained alert, however, peering in our direction, using their sense of sight, hearing and smell to warn them of any approach. Once or

Warri and Yatungka in their camp at Ngarinarri.

twice we moved a short distance towards them and in a flash they disappeared into the bush again.

During the night I woke frequently, troubled by the knowledge that we were to be responsible for removing the last nomads from the desert, and on each occasion I heard Warri and Yatungka speaking quietly to each other. What were they talking about? Perhaps they knew that once they left Ngarinarri they would probably never return to their own country again. Or were they discussing what Mudjon had told them — that there would be no action taken against them when they reached Wiluna? Perhaps they were having second thoughts about leaving, preferring to remain in the desert. If that was the case we would be placed in a most difficult situation. Could we just drive off and leave them to die at Ngarinarri?

Chapter Fifteen

I woke early to find that Mudjon had already paid a visit to Warri and Yatungka. He, too, was concerned that they may have decided not to leave Ngarinarri, but was relieved to find they were eager to move out as soon as we were ready.

Before departing we considered it fitting to indicate to whoever might pass by Ngarinarri in the future, that the last nomads of the Mandildjara tribe were found in the vicinity and, to denote that fact, we erected a cairn of limestone on the southern edge of the claypan, about seventy metres south of the well and about forty-five metres north of the camp that Warri and Yatungka had occupied for so long under such appalling conditions. Inside the cairn we placed a bottle containing a letter with some details about the Aboriginal couple. A mulga pole, two and a half metres in length, was inserted into the cairn and to this was wired a stainless steel plate on which we had punched out the name of the waterhole and the date, and indicated that Warri and Yatungka had been found nearby and had been taken to Wiluna.

The time had arrived for the nomads to part with the dogs which had been their sole companions for several years. Mudjon informed them they would be unable to take the animals as they

Warri and Yatungka prepare to leave Ngarinarri and their land forever.

were classified as vermin and would be destroyed as soon as we reached station country. I wondered what their chances were of surviving without their Aboriginal masters to procure water for them. It was impossible for them to obtain water at the well, they had relied on Yatungka to draw it for them. In their emaciated condition they would be unable to travel far in search of water and I doubted whether they would survive.

It should be recalled that on a previous occasion, Warri had refused to leave the desert when he realised that to do so would have meant parting with his beloved animals, but on this occasion, when Mudjon broached the subject with him, there was no argument and he accepted without hesitation that the dogs must remain at Ngarinarri. They were nowhere to be seen that morning, having disappeared as soon as we began to stir, but I was certain they were observing our every move from the surrounding scrub.

Yatungka appeared more concerned than Warri about the future of the animals. She climbed down the well for the last time, collecting a little water which she poured into the dish on the surface. The dogs would have sufficient to sustain them for a day or two, but after that time they would have to fend for themselves.

We were now ready to leave and Mudjon advised the couple, who gathered together a few possessions, their spears and spear thrower, a carrying dish, an axe and a few cans, and walked towards the vehicle without a backward glance at the camp where they had spent so many anxious days. They did not look for, or shout a farewell to their dogs, the animals that had wandered up and down the country with them, had hunted for them, and provided some warmth during the bitterly cold nights in the desert. They appeared to have been already forgotten but, as Mudjon later informed me, such was not the case. Although they loved the animals they had accepted the fact that the dogs must remain and there was nothing to be gained by any form of demonstration, either of affection for them or in opposition to the decision to leave them at Ngarinarri.

Once more we experienced considerable difficulty in getting Warri into the vehicle. He was clearly terrified, making feeble efforts to climb up but he trembled so violently that he was forced to abandon each attempt. Yatungka, on the other hand, was eager to get into the vehicle and clambered up without hesitation, calling to Warri to redouble his efforts, that there was no reason to be afraid.

Mudjon, too, shouted encouragement to his old friend, and with much vocal urging and with our physical assistance Warri finally managed to get onto the truck. Both he and Yatungka refused to sit upright, insisting that they be allowed to lie down, and we therefore arranged a bed of blankets on the floor of the vehicle. They also asked that they be completely covered, so we spread a tarpaulin over them.

Mudjon pacifying Warri and Yatungka
who were terrified of the noise of the vehicle.

We requested Mudjon, who usually rode in the cabin of the vehicle, to ride in the back, for he would be required to allay their fears and to relay any requests they might have during the journey.

Slowly we drove away from the waterhole, the home of the last nomads of the Mandildjara. It was, indeed, a moving moment. Ngarinarri, which had seen many of the desert people over the centuries, had perhaps seen its last Aborigines — for it was doubtful that any would pass that way again. The last of a people who once proudly roamed their country and who could survive where no white man could live, now lay huddled beneath the canvas in a state of terror. What was terrifying them at that moment was not the presence of white men, for they had been in contact with them on previous occasions, not the judgement of the people that may have awaited them when they reached

Wiluna, it was the roaring, bouncing monster which tossed them about as they clung to each other beneath the covers.

We had barely started our journey when muffled sounds, which became progressively louder, issued from under the canvas. We must stop, said Mudjon, for Warri wished to urinate, the matter was most urgent. The tarpaulin was peeled back to allow the man to climb down. I felt we would have trouble in inducing him to return to the vehicle but after standing about for a short time he willingly climbed up and disappeared under the cover again. That procedure occurred many times during the first few kilometres of travel, the cold weather and Warri's state of extreme anxiety being responsible for this.

Yatungka had taken the morning's happenings extremely well and appeared much more adaptable to the rather frightening conditions in which the couple were placed. She played a very significant part in comforting Warri, although it was necessary for Mudjon to support her with a continual patter of soothing words.

On one occasion a halt was called because Warri had developed a severe headache. He demanded that the traditional Aboriginal treatment for the complaint should be implemented and I tied a strip of cloth around his head, but no matter how tightly it was drawn it was never tight enough, a little more tension was always required.

Travelling was much easier and quicker than on the outward journey as we followed our tracks, the easiest path across the sandhills being clearly delineated, and we reached Wangabaddi at noon. We intended having lunch there and the cover was drawn from Warri and Yatungka, who, blinking in the sudden brightness could scarcely believe that they had travelled from Ngarinarri to Wangabaddi in what was, to them, an incredibly short period of time.

Warri muttered something to Mudjon, then moved off into the bush, to return after a few minutes with a bundle of spears which he had cached away on a previous visit. The weapons were of good quality, lovingly made, very straight and each shaft was two and a half to three metres in length, some having barbed tips. These were of two kinds: one having the barb as an integral part of the shaft, fashioned at the time of manufacture; with the other type the barb had been made separately and had then been bound to the shaft with kangaroo sinew.

It had been Warri's custom to leave a supply of weapons at several waterholes throughout the desert, to be used whilst he remained in a particular area then stored away until he returned at a later time. But although visitors to Mandildjara country were infrequent he took the precaution of hiding the spears well away from the well, ensuring that they would be there when he came again.

We were now armed to the teeth, carrying over twenty spears. Those weapons were very precious to Warri and Mudjon, they represented status and would be displayed for all to see when we reached Wiluna.

The bundle, previously noted at Wangabaddi, still nestled in the tree where we had replaced it after examination on the outward journey, and I once more broached the subject with Mudjon, who questioned Warri about its contents. After a lengthy conversation Mudjon advised there was nothing sinister about the bundle at all. Long ago, when game was fairly plentiful Warri had hunted down a kangaroo in the vicinity. He and Yatungka and the dogs had eaten their fill and to prevent his animals from choking on the small bones that were left he had wrapped the remains in canvas and placed them in the mulga tree, well out of reach. The mystery at Wangabaddi had been solved!

As we prepared to leave Wangabaddi, Mudjon walked over to Warri and Yatungka, who had elected to sit in the open near the well, about twenty-seven metres from where we had lunched, and informed them we were almost ready to depart. They both rose shakily to their feet and we witnessed a most touching scene as

Warri walked away for a short distance in the opposite direction to stand and gaze about, as though having one last look at the place he had visited so often when his people had moved about the country, the place where there had been much jubilation when the hunt was successful and his people ate well, and where, in recent sad times, he and Yatungka had struggled so hard to exist in a drought-stricken land.

It was a moving moment, not only for Warri but for all who observed that action. Warri knew he would never return and I felt that Wangabaddi had seen its last Aborigine, that never again would the desert people take their drinking water from the well and that after several thousand years of occupation by the Mandildjara, the only sounds that would be heard there in future would be the wind rustling the leaves of the mulga trees. It was unlikely that human voices would ever be heard at Wangabaddi again.

On our arrival back at the depot we quickly reloaded the vehicles as we intended to reach the well at Kata Kata before nightfall. There were no animal tracks in the area we had cleared as a precaution against fire, a further indication of the extent to which the long drought had depleted the desert fauna.

During the long haul from Kata Kata to Wangabaddi and return we had not seen a single kangaroo, emu or goanna, and there was an almost complete absence of any form of bird life. The country was dead and would take a very long time to recover after the drought had ended.

We had seen one rather emaciated kangaroo in the hills above Kata Kata on the outward journey, the first we had observed since leaving Moongooloo. How it managed to survive without water and without any succulent grass to provide some moisture, defies explanation. There had not been one night when dew fell in the whole period we had been in the desert, and the birds and animals were denied even that source of water.

We reached Kata Kata in the late afternoon and Warri and

Yatungka soon had a fire blazing in their camp about thirty metres away. Mudjon, in the process of breaking down a small dry tree nearby for firewood, found a large lizard in the hollow trunk, and what great excitement there was as he and Warri extracted it from its hiding place. In a twinkling Yatungka had the unfortunate reptile cooking in the hot ashes and within twenty minutes it had been devoured — head, legs and all — accompanied by grunts of ecstasy. It had been a long time since they had tasted such a delicacy.

We studied our maps that evening to plan our homeward journey. Our fuel supplies were low and it was necessary to plot the most economical route out of the desert. We decided that, should our fuel position become critical, we would transfer all the petrol to one vehicle which would then proceed to Glenayle Station to obtain supplies.

We wished to travel with all speed to Wiluna for Warri and Yatungka were in urgent need of medical attention. There were two feasible routes to follow from Kata Kata. We could run east to a track which ran north from the so-called 'Gunbarrel Highway', and having reached that point we could turn south and increase our speed considerably. That route however was the long way home and it was unlikely that we would have sufficient fuel for such an undertaking.

The alternative was to proceed due south over trackless country to the 'Gunbarrel'. It was the shorter route but sand ridges would have to be crossed which would slow our progress and increase our fuel consumption. It was the route favoured by Mudjon, who expressed his desire to visit some waterholes that lay out in that direction for nostalgic reasons, and because Warri had cached more weapons at several of them. So south we would go to please the two old desert men.

Chapter Sixteen

That night at Kata Kata was bitterly cold, with a strong wind blowing from the south-east, and Warri and Yatungka, despite their several fires, were uncomfortable without the warmth they normally obtained from their dogs. It was possibly the first time in their lives they had slept, or rather attempted to sleep, without a dingo or two nestling against their bodies, and I had no doubt that the animals they had left at Ngarinarri were also ill at ease that night without the company of the humans with whom they had been so closely associated for so long.

Warri was a pitiful sight when I visited the camp at sunrise with a breakfast of hot tea, eggs and toast prepared by Harry Lever who, morning, noon and night, was able to prepare meals, often under the most difficult conditions. Warri was miserable; he was cold, he felt ill, and copious draughts of tea did little to improve his condition. In his emaciated state he was no longer able to tolerate low temperatures, and he shivered violently. Desert Aborigines were renowned for their ability to live through the bitterly cold nights of the desert without any form of clothing, and without animals skins for covering, relying solely on their little fires and their animals for warmth. But a man in Warri's physical condition had little resistance to the cold.

Once more we experienced difficulty in getting him into the vehicle. He insisted on firing some patches of spinifex and it was not until he had warmed himself that we were able to get him on board. After covering him with blankets and canvas and making sure that he felt comfortable, we proceeded in a south-westerly direction to cross some stony ridges a little to the west of Kata Kata, then ran out along a valley to the south-east.

We noticed a cave in the breakaway country about one hundred and sixty metres above the valley floor, and climbing up to investigate found a large nest of the stick nest rat (*Leporillis apicalis*) which extended into the depths of the cave. That type of country was favoured by the rat, as the loose shale provided the material it required to build its substantial residence. We had encountered a great number of nests in previous travels in the desert, many of which appeared to be of fairly recent construction, but had never seen the creature nor had we observed its tracks. It had obviously been present in considerable numbers in the past, but is now believed to be extinct, its demise being attributed, in part, to the feral cats that are now found throughout the desert regions of the country.

The stick nest rat built its home of shale and sticks, firmly cementing the material together with an extremely hard substance which would appear to be a mixture of urine and faeces. Whatever the mortar is composed of it exudes an overbearing stench when disturbed and presumably it was designed as a protective measure against predators. Even without such protection the creature would have been relatively safe inside its nest, as the stone and stick construction is almost indestructible and no animal that inhabited the desert would have been able to penetrate it.

I have always found it hard to believe that the rat has been extinct for a great many years on the Australian mainland when so many of the nests give the impression that they are of fairly recent origin, and the twigs used in the manufacture often appear to have only recently been bitten off. However, the fresh appearance of those nests possibly stems from the fact that they are usually to be found in the depths of caves, protected from the strong sunlight, desert winds and infrequent rains.

Some nests have been built vertically, while others are more horizontal, following crevices and openings in the rock face. They were initially constructed to accommodate one pair but were added to at intervals as the family increased, and several generations often lived in one nest. The formidable construction protected the burrow which extended below ground for a considerable distance, but despite nature's efforts to protect the stick nest rat, it is now thought to be extinct except for a colony on an island off the South Australian coast.

We continued on past Walloogoobal and, after crossing the first of the sand ridges, turned to the south-south-west for, in that direction lay Yoodalbooroo rock hole, a place both Warri and Mudjon wished to visit. After several kilometres Mudjon drew my attention to a large bloodwood tree which rose high above the scrub ahead. It was a most impressive tree and had been a landmark for the desert people as they moved across the country. Mudjon indicated that it meant far more to his people than just a navigational aid. It was revered by them because, like the stones at Wangabaddi and Walloogoobal, it was the work of Warrida who had planted the tree long ago as he travelled the land and that, said Mudjon, was why the tree had grown so tall.

On closer inspection we observed that the trunk displayed some rather unusual features. On one side there were irregularities which I thought might represent male genital organs, and on the opposite side there was an opening which suggested an anus. I inquired of Mudjon whether my interpretation was correct and whether it was the presence of those features that had caused the tree to have so much significance to the Aboriginal people. He replied that my assumption 'might be' and I suspect that it was the anatomy of the trunk rather than the size of the tree that first attracted the attention of the desert dwellers.

Sixteen kilometres across spinifex plains and low sand ridges brought us to Djunbaroongu rock hole. Strangely, both Warri and Mudjon had difficulty in locating it, requesting us to stop at frequent intervals while they surveyed the countryside in an attempt to orientate themselves. I wondered why, after navigating between other waterholes without effort, there was some confusion concerning the position of Djunbaroongu. Mudjon indicated that it lay in one direction whilst Warri pointed in another, and both insisted that their course was the right one. However, I felt that Warri and Yatungka, having been regular visitors to the waterhole for many years, would be in a better position to locate it, and Mudjon eventually agreed and we drove directly to the well without any further delay or hesitation under Warri's guidance.

Djunbaroongu rock hole was situated on a stony flat amongst a few mulga trees and, as expected, contained no water. Warrida had been there before us, leaving his visiting card, the white stones, nearby.

We reached the top of a low range after travelling another nine and a half kilometres and then spent considerable time and effort in finding a path down the thickly wooded southern slope to the open spinifex plain below. Fallen timber was removed and overhanging branches cut away until we had cleared a track that could be negotiated without damage to the vehicles or their occupants. Warri and Yatungka appeared unperturbed and seemingly uninterested in our feverish activity and rode down the steep hillside as though such things happened every day of their lives.

Warri's fear of the vehicles had abated considerably and he now appeared to be enjoying the experience. For fifty or sixty years the only way known to him of getting from one place to another was on foot, and now he was able to sit in reasonable comfort, several centimetres above the ground and watch the spinifex and scrub gliding by. Yatungka had revelled in it almost from the outset. It was easier travelling in that fashion than trudging through the needle-sharp clumps of spinifex, carrying weapons and implements that were required for their hunting and food-gathering activities.

We crossed a wide plain to make camp in the scrub at its southern edge. Both Warri and Yatungka were happy as they climbed down from the vehicle, for they were anticipating a meal of their favourite food.

During the course of the day Mudjon had seen a kangaroo and drew Warri and Yatungka's attention to it. They were greatly excited and Warri's instinctive reaction was to crouch whilst he assessed the situation.

We were reluctant to molest the animal for we felt that if it could survive under the conditions that had prevailed for so long in the desert it deserved to be left unharmed. Mudjon turned a deaf ear to our argument, insisting that Warri and Yatungka were in urgent need of kangaroo meat and they would obtain much greater benefit from it than from all the canned meat and damper that we could offer them.

After the unfortunate animal had been killed Mudjon disembowelled it and, tying the legs together with a length of intestine, hoisted it onto his shoulders to carry it in the manner of his ancestors. Warri and Yatungka were ecstatic at the thought of eating *malu* again and immediately we halted to make camp Mudjon proceeded to prepare the feast.

A pit was dug, a fire was made in the bottom and when the earth had been heated sufficiently the coals were raked out and the animal, fur and all, was thrown in. Earth was shovelled over it until only the front paws and back legs were visible and the coals were then heaped on top. In a very short time Mudjon announced

Warri, sick and miserable at the camp near Kata Kata.

that all was ready, the animal was 'cooked', and giving it a quick tug he had it out of the pit and the dismemberment began. The fur was only slightly singed but Mudjon was adamant that the *malu* was just right for eating, even though the flesh was barely cooked near the surface, the remainder being quite raw. Warri and Yatungka could scarcely contain themselves whilst Mudjon was engaged in the butchering and immediately that process had been completed they fell upon the mounds of raw meat, consuming a great amount and emitting little groans of pleasure at intervals. There would be a short pause and then they would renew their attack on the rapidly diminishing meat supply. They had not eaten so well for many months and I was concerned about the rapidity of eating and the quantity consumed as I felt that the food should be rationed, that it should be eaten slowly and only in small portions initially lest they develop problems in their digestive systems which had long been unaccustomed to this type of food. But there was no hope of convincing Warri and Yatungka of this. The *malu* was there and it was to be eaten and nothing would prevent them from having their fill. It was, said Mudjon, 'good tucker' for them, and he agreed with the feelings of an old Aboriginal man of the Broome area who once told me there was 'nothing like kangaroo to put strength into you'. However, Mudjon himself ate little of the meat, preferring 'white man's tucker' of tinned meat, vegetables, damper and tea.

I spoke with Mudjon at great length that evening. It would be the last night that he and Warri and Yatungka would spend in their own country for the next day we would be below the southern border of the Mandildjara homeland.

Mudjon again talked of the reasons why Warri and Yatungka had elected to remain in the desert, he chuckled as he recalled that memorable fight at Birrill, he referred once more to the time when his people moved across the desert, following the unmarked path, the 'wongai main road' as he called it. He expressed his sadness that those days had gone forever, that the black man had disappeared from the desert. The country was 'finished', it was dead, the final blow being delivered by the long drought that now ravaged the land.

As I looked at the three Aboriginal people I wondered whether they would ever return to their country, whether that night was to be the very last they would spend in the land their people had occupied for so many thousand years. Were they the last Mandildjaras to leave their footprints in the soil of their homeland? I felt that I was witnessing the end of an era; that despite Mudjon's assertion that one day he would lead his people back into the desert, Aboriginal people would never walk that land again.

Chapter Seventeen

Our journey continued towards Yoodalbooroo rock hole, through mulga thickets and spinifex plains. After travelling nine and a half kilometres Mudjon called a halt. He was confused, stating that we should have reached the waterhole but it was nowhere in sight. We changed course, running a little over a kilometre and a half to the south-east, emerging onto a low stony rise, when Mudjon requested that we remain there whilst he reconnoitred on foot to the north-east. Should he locate the well a 'smoke' would be sent up and we were then to proceed in that direction by vehicle.

As we waited for the signal, Warri walked to a mulga tree a short distance away and, plucking some bark from the trunk, he returned to make a small fire, converting the bark to a white ash. He then crushed the now dry and brittle leaves of the native tobacco plant which had been collected by Mudjon many days previously and, mixing this material with the ash, he threw a handful into his mouth, chewing vigorously for a minute or two then spitting out the masticated mass which was then placed above an ear for future use. The whole process was repeated several times until he had fashioned a substantial wad of 'chewing tobacco', enough to last him for some days.

Warri appeared to enjoy the 'tobacco', and it was probably the first time he had had the real thing for a long period. The wad that we observed above his ear on the day we met him at Ngarinarri was, in all probability, some type of substitute, for we did not observe any plants growing along the 'main road', the path down which Warri and Yatungka moved.

Mudjon, strangely enough, was not interested in chewing the tobacco and apparently collected it for the use of his kinsfolk in Wiluna. However, at the rate Warri chewed I doubted whether there would be any left when we reached the end of our journey.

A 'smoke' rose above the scrub to the north-east, indicating that Mudjon had located the waterhole, and in a kilometre we reached Yoodalbooroo, a rock hole situated in undulating, gravelly country amongst a few scattered mulga trees. The opening was about half a metre by one and a half metres with a depth of one and a half metres, and although no water was visible at the bottom, the soil was moist, so perhaps some digging would have met with success. However we had no desire to obtain water at Yoodalbooroo, for a camel, possibly crazed with thirst, had fallen into the well and being unable to extricate itself had died an agonising death, and its bleached bones lay at the bottom of the well.

Whilst Warri and Mudjon squatted at the edge of the well discussing the fate of the camel, Yatungka slipped away to the east, returning with a bundle of spears which had been cached in a mulga tree. There were ten spears in all: some barbed, some plain, many decorated with lines that had been laboriously cut into the wood with a knife or cutting stone. The weapons, said Mudjon, had been made long ago when the seasons were kind, when Warri and Yatungka had spent a considerable period of time at this waterhole.

To the people of the Mandildjara, Yoodalbooroo was of great significance for it was the last camping place of Warrida before he met his death, forty-eight kilometres away to the south. For Mudjon, too, the place had memories; he had camped there many times when he roamed the desert and he insisted on showing us the spot where, long ago, he had cooked a kangaroo. He pointed out a mulga tree from which he had once cut a slab of wood to be later fashioned into a spear thrower, and after searching the ground in the vicinity of the tree he was overjoyed to find a large piece of timber which, he said, he had split from the main slab whilst making the spear thrower. Mudjon possessed an amazing memory and appeared never to forget even the most trifling event. To be able to recall, after a period of thirty or forty years, where he had made a fire, had eaten quandongs or had sent up smoke was incredible.

We continued our journey to the south-south-west, passing through dense thickets of mulga and over wide spinifex plains to reach a low stony rise which extended for several kilometres in an east-west direction. Only a few sandhills were visible away to the south and we therefore anticipated making good progress throughout the afternoon, but when we eventually reached the sand ridges we found them to be impassable and were forced to run out to the east for several kilometres, making camp for the night amongst the dunes.

Warri and Yatungka dined well on the remains of the kangaroo, supplemented by food from our larder, and seemed to be contented. They had eaten kangaroo for breakfast, lunch and dinner, with occasional nibbles in between. After the muddy water of Ngarinarri, the only fluid they had drunk for several weeks, the tea we supplied, which contained copious amounts of milk, was greatly appreciated. They had travelled well during the day, becoming accustomed to the movement and noise of the vehicle, and their physical condition showed some improvement, the result of the high protein and high calorie diet they had been having over the previous few days.

Although they showed no outward signs of anxiety concerning their reception in Wiluna, I am sure they were apprehensive, despite Mudjon's assurance that no harm would befall them. I wondered how they would react to living once more amongst a group of their own people after so many years of solitude in the desert.

The next morning, still unable to cross the sandhill that barred our way to the south, we moved to the east-south-east until we reached the eastern extremity of the sand ridges, then turned to run south through a wide plain of high spinifex. I had noticed in the past that whenever we encountered spinifex of that type, Mudjon had an almost irresistible urge to fire it. He was irritated by it and obtained great satisfaction in setting it alight, and that occasion was no exception. He wished to burn the country although there was no earthly reason for doing so when we did not wish to signal anybody, we did not have any desire to flush out any game that may have been lurking in the grass and there was no purpose in regenerating the land as it was highly unlikely that any Aboriginal people would walk that country again. Mudjon wished to burn because it was almost an instinctive action; something he had learnt in the years he had spent in the desert and which was not forgotten overnight!

We restrained him from taking this action, pointing out that the vehicles would be in great danger should the breeze increase in velocity or change direction, and that we did not wish to walk the remaining distance to Glenayle Station. The grunts and low mutterings that issued from the man as we progressed through the tall grass, however, indicated that he was far from happy with our decision.

The open country gave way to dense mulga scrub which hindered our progress, and I was interested to note that a great number of trees were dead. As there was no evidence they had been burnt I could only assume that they had been victims of the great drought. If these, the hardiest of trees, had died through lack of moisture, how could an elderly Aboriginal couple survive in the desert for so long under such appalling conditions?

We emerged from the scrub to see the first sign of civilisation we had encountered since leaving the Stock Route, a manmade track that extended in an east-west direction to the horizon, the Gunbarrel Highway. After several hundred kilometres of bouncing over spinifex clumps, grinding over sandhills and crashing through scrub the Highway, a single track gouged and rutted by washaways, was a most welcome sight.

The track was made by Len Beadell and his party in the early 1960s and extends for several hundred kilometres from the Western Australian border to Carnegie Station, crossing some of the most isolated country in Australia, with no permanent waterholes or petrol pumps along the way to assist the traveller. The track was one of several made by Beadell through the Gibson and Great Sandy Deserts in connection with the rocket range at Woomera in South Australia and the monitoring station at Talgamo on the coast of Western Australia between Port Hedland and Broome.

In recent years the track has been used by adventurous — and sometimes foolhardy — people who choose to travel in out-of-the-way places. The journey over the Gunbarrel is not to be taken lightly for a breakdown could mean death as several weeks may pass before another traveller makes the crossing.

A few years ago two young men, ignoring warnings of the dangers involved, attempted to travel the Highway from west to east in a sports car. They left Carnegie Station with inadequate supplies of water and food in a car entirely unsuitable for the type of track that had to be negotiated. About one hundred and sixty kilometres out in the desert the vehicle refused to go any further. They were stranded with insufficient water to allow them to walk back to Carnegie and were indeed fortunate that a four-wheel-drive vehicle travelling from the east came upon them, and two

Warri and Yatungka gazing in wonder at the first windmill on their way out of the desert. Never had they seen so much water and so many kangaroo tracks.

very relieved young men were transported to safety, leaving the sports car out on the track to be recovered at a later date.

Warri and Yatungka emerged from under the covers to gaze in wonder at the road. Many times they had crossed the narrow, and sometimes indistinct tracks that meandered through their country, but they were nothing compared to the Gunbarrel. Mudjon informed them that we would follow the 'road' all the way to Wiluna, that we would not have to bounce over the spinifex or grind over sandhills any more, that sort of travelling was behind us.

We drove westwards, avoiding as many of the old washaways as possible, to reach a trig point just south of the track where we lunched on the summit. Warri took the opportunity to again burn some mulga bark, the ash remaining being mixed with the dry 'tobacco', the *wamma*, to make a supply of chewing tobacco to last for the remainder of the journey. Both he and Yatungka were cheerful and ate heartily, squatting amongst the stones on that desolate hill, seemingly unperturbed that soon they would meet the elders in Wiluna, the people they had offended so long ago. Perhaps they did not realise that the time of that meeting was so close.

Forty-eight kilometres further on we reached the first windmill, Watertree Well on Carnegie Station. Warri climbed down from the vehicle and was quite overwhelmed by the great number of animal and bird tracks so clearly visible in the soft soil around the well. To a man whose life depended on observing tracks and following them for the kill, it was all so confusing. He had never seen so much evidence of game before and could not take his eyes off the ground, exclaiming '*malu, malu*' many times.

A breeze had sprung up, the fan of the mill was rotating freely and water was being pumped into a large tank which was almost full. It was the first water we had seen since leaving Moongooloo and it was a beautiful sight. We encouraged Warri to stand on a rail in order that he could see the great volume of water in the

Warri and Mudjon.

tank, and on peering over the rim and seeing more water than he had seen, possibly for years, he reeled back in amazement shouting '*kapi* (water)' and had to be supported to prevent him falling over with shock. It was all very confusing for the desert man and woman who had seen precious little water in recent times.

Twenty-one kilometres to the west we reached the deserted Carnegie Station homestead, the first building we had seen since leaving Glenayle over three weeks previously. Warri and Yatungka displayed considerable interest in the house and outbuildings, and were highly amused to see their travelling companions, both white and Aboriginal, washing the dust of the desert from their bodies.

Refreshed, we drove a few kilometres to the north to camp in the vicinity of Mount Bates, a low range named by John Forrest during his 1874 expedition from Geraldton, on the Western Australian coast, to the Overland Telegraph Line in South Australia. Forrest blazed a tree nearby, and as we were unable to locate it on the previous expedition we intended to search once more in the hope of locating it.

Although the night was cold with a breeze coming from the south-east, for some inexplicable reason both Warri and Yatungka shed the clothes we had given them, and I wondered whether they were having some regrets about their decision to leave Ngarinarri, that they were already homesick for the desert. Not so, said Mudjon. They felt uncomfortable wearing the white man's shirts and trousers and, with their several small fires, were quite happy to sit naked as they had done throughout their years in the desert.

The breeze strengthened during the night, whipping the dust along before it, there being little vegetation to hold the soil down, and we were pleased when daylight came and we could begin our search for Forrest's tree.

We were looking for a corkwood tree carrying the inscription 'F 52' (Forrest's fifty-second camp from Geraldton) and, guided by the explorer's description of the locality and crossbearings taken twenty years later, we were able to pinpoint the position of the tree which, sadly, had disappeared; the result of fire, termites or just old age!

We continued on to Glenayle Station where, as usual, a hearty welcome was extended by Henry and Mrs Ward, who were most interested to hear of our exploits. Stan Gratte had made contact with them on several occasions via the Royal Flying Doctor Service radio, and consequently they had some knowledge of our movements since leaving the station.

They told us of a woman who, with several camels for companions, had travelled over the Gunbarrel Highway from the Northern Territory. She had rested at Glenayle for a few days and had departed for Wiluna a day or two before our arrival. She was on her way to the coast to achieve a long-standing ambition to take her camels across the desert country of Western Australia. Mudjon had noticed her tracks and those of the animals when we emerged out onto the Highway from the desert. Her remarkable journey was only possible through determination and courage and I pay tribute to the 'Camel Lady'.

Mudjon, with Warri and Yatungka, made camp amongst mulga trees near the homestead and set about the task of cooking an emu which Mudjon had killed during the day. Again, a pit was dug, a fire lit, the coals were raked out and the bird was placed in the depression to be covered with earth, and the fire then raked over the top. The cooking process was to go on for several hours at low heat and the bird was not removed until the following morning.

We left Glenayle for Wiluna via Lorna Glen, where we intended to search for a tree that had been blazed in 1896. With the assistance of the station manager we were successful in locating the tree, and we camped for the night a short distance from it.

Warri and Yatungka quickly lit their fire nearby, eager to dine on the emu. They had put their clothes on again, and Yatungka was in a happy mood. This was to be the last night we would spend with our friends from the desert and with Mudjon, and I was saddened by the thought that next morning we would part company.

Warri was quiet after he and Yatungka had eaten and I wondered whether he was becoming a little apprehensive for, on the morrow, he would, for the first time in a great many years, come face to face with the Mandildjara elders and, despite Mudjon's assurances that no harm would come to him or to Yatungka, I was sure he feared that meeting. I think each member of our party, both black and white, went to bed that night wondering what the reception would be amongst the Aboriginal community of Wiluna when we drove in from the desert.

Chapter Eighteen

Warri was unwell that night at Lorna Glen and I believe the diet he had been enjoying for several days was more than his weakened gastro-intestinal system could tolerate. He refused to eat at breakfast, disappearing into the bush at intervals. Mudjon suggested that it was not the 'tucker' that was causing the problem but the fact that within a few hours he would come face to face with his people, the people he had offended and, said Mudjon, Warri was 'very worried'.

Mudjon, too, was not himself as we prepared to depart on the last leg of our journey. He was irritable and non-communicative, and in response to my question as to what was troubling him he stated that he would never 'go bush' again; he was too old and too tired to travel about the country. However, I felt that the real reason for his depression was that he, like Warri, was most concerned about the welcome they would receive that day.

We reached Wiluna a little before midday and, as we drove through the town, little groups of people stared silently at the two desert people sitting immobile in the rear of the vehicle. Our first stop was the nursing post and within moments of our arrival many Aboriginal people came from all directions, the word that the two old people had come in from the desert had spread rapidly and all were interested in seeing them as soon as possible.

Warri and Yatungka remained in the vehicle with their eyes downcast as they were scrutinised intently by those who gathered around, and for a long time not a word was spoken. There were no greetings, no shouts of joy, in fact there was no sign of recognition on either side, and yet the sons of Warri and Yatungka were within a few metres of their parents. The only evidence of the intense emotions being experienced were the tears streaming down Warri's cheeks and on the cheeks of many others in that gathering. There was no feeling of hostility towards the couple. The people were overcome because Warri and Yatungka had been found alive and because of their emaciated condition. They only stared incredulously and muttered 'poor fella' over and over again.

It was a moving scene, not only for Aborigines but for the white people who were present. One sensed the tremendous feeling of relief amongst the people that the old couple had survived, but it was tinged with sadness as they noted the frail bodies and realised that Warri and Yatungka were in a precarious state of health. Mudjon told the gathering of the search through the desert, of the meeting at Ngarinarri and of the events since that time, whilst the old couple sat motionless, glancing neither to left nor right.

We considered that it would be inadvisable to keep Warri and Yatungka at the nursing post, that it was preferable to obtain medication there and then to take them to the camp where Mudjon and his wife and their kinsfolk could care for them. To keep the couple shut up in a hospital room at that time would possibly have had a deleterious effect on them. They needed the company of their own people who would minister to them.

We drove out of town to the Reserve where Warri and Yatungka, with their few possessions, were to take up residence.

They appeared confused in their new surroundings, sitting amongst their own people once more. They found communication difficult, for the years they had spent alone in the desert had tended to stifle their ability to converse in the normal way.

It was a sad moment for us as we bade farewell to our Aboriginal friends. I hoped I would have Mudjon's company and his guidance on future journeys into the desert and I looked forward to the time when we would meet again, little knowing that that meeting would take place under rather tragic circumstances. I knew he would do everything in his power to assist Warri and Yatungka adjust to a new way of life, to soften the impact of civilisation on them and to ensure that adequate clothing and shelter was provided.

Mudjon spoke again of leading his people back into the desert, back into their own country and away from what he saw as the destructive effects of the white man's mode of living and his alcohol. He requested that I approach 'the government' to make a plea for the establishment of a permanent water at Yildgee claypan in Mandildjara country, where he and his people could be assured of water in even the most severe drought. I promised that I would undertake the task, it was the least I could do for a man who displayed the utmost concern for his people, but I felt that even if a water supply was provided it was most unlikely that he would recruit many who would follow him home.

It was sad, too, to farewell Warri and Yatungka as they sat on the bare earth of the Reserve surrounded by their belongings, the things they had treasured, things so necessary in their fight for survival in the desert. The nomads of the Western Gibson had rejoined their people after the years of exile and ostracism, but it was a vastly different society to that which they had known in the years before their elopement.

How would they cope in a strange world, how would they adjust to the presence of other human beings? At least they were assured of food and water, it would no longer be necessary to dig deep into the earth in the search for water, nor to walk vast distances to obtain sufficient food. Medical attention would be provided during any illness, and life for Warri and Yatungka would be much easier.

It would be easier, but would it be happier? After years of roaming the desert, hunting and food gathering, using all the skills they had learnt in order to survive, the inactive life of the Reserve dweller would possibly be a boring and depressive existence.

We could only hope they would enjoy the time that was left to them. With adequate food and proper medical attention, I felt that they would recover from their ordeal, and perhaps participate to some extent in the day-to -day affairs of the people. But should they pine for their country and express a wish to return there, one would be faced with a most unenviable decision. To take them back to Ngarinarri, to leave them there alone once more, would be to leave them to die within a few weeks if the drought continued. Not to accede to their wishes would be to deny them their right to choose where they should live and where they should die. I fervently hoped that nobody would be required to make that decision.

We drove away from the Reserve waving goodbye to a unique man and woman, the last of the nomads. A chapter in our history had concluded, it was the end of an era.

Epilogue

In the weeks that followed their arrival in Wiluna it was found necessary to send Warri and Yatungka to the hospital at Meekatharra, a move they accepted surprisingly well. However they remained as inseparable as they had been during the long years in the desert, reluctant to let each other out of sight. With good food and medical treatment administered by my good friend, Dr L Haris, they made an excellent recovery and were once more able to join their people in Wiluna.

Warri did not appear to comprehend what was happening to his people. He saw that much of the law was openly disregarded, especially by the young, the social organisation was disintegrating rapidly and the widespread abuse of alcohol was destroying the self-respect and self-reliance his people once possessed. He saw how Mudjon strove to maintain the traditions, how he attempted to instill in the young people a pride in being a Mandildjara, or a Budidjara — of being Aboriginal — but it was a losing battle.

In the following months Warri and Yatungka seemed to be reasonably happy, never openly expressing any desire to return to Ngarinarri. Warri rarely spoke, content to sit for long periods of time before his fire, whilst Yatungka, as she overcame her shyness and her fear of tribal retribution, took a more active part in the affairs of the people. She never moved far from her husband's side and when engaged in conversation with others would, from time to time, reach out to touch Warri as though to reassure him that she was near, that he was not forgotten.

Mudjon continued his efforts to maintain and, to some extent, revive the culture of the desert people. He travelled far and wide to attend meetings concerned with the law at Jigalong, Warburton and other places. He organised the initiation of young men, the rite of passage to manhood.

A few months after our return from the desert, Mudjon became ill and was sent south to Perth for major surgery. I visited him on many occasions whilst he was in hospital and was saddened by what I saw. My old friend was a broken man, no longer able to talk and could communicate only by signs. He had never learnt to read or write and could not express himself in any way once he had lost the power of speech. His days were spent idly thumbing through magazines, gazing at print which had no meaning for him.

He indicated to me his desire to go home to Wiluna as soon as possible for he was unhappy in the strange world of the hospital ward, he wished to see his own people again.

I wondered how an elder, a man intent on leading his people back to their traditional ways would be able to communicate, to pass on his ideas in future. Perhaps he considered that the loss of speech was only a temporary thing and that with the passage of time he would once more be able to talk, but having obtained the medical facts I knew that it was not possible for him to ever conduct a normal conversation again. Even with prolonged training, which would require a long period away from his people and which I knew he would not accept, he would recover only a portion of his speech.

On my last visit before he returned home I was deeply moved

as we shook hands. I felt I was seeing my old friend for the last time, and that never again would I have the privilege of his companionship on journeys into the desert when he would pass on his knowledge of his people and their customs and teach me of the love he had for his country.

Mudjon died shortly afterwards at Wiluna, and I lost a very dear friend, a man whom I had come to admire. He was buried in the local cemetery, far from the resting place of his ancestors, and with his death went his dream of leading his people back to their homeland.

Perhaps a fitting epitaph for such a dignified and remarkable man was the notice inserted in a newspaper following his death.

MUDJON: A tribute to a great man of the Mandildjara who strove to uphold the traditions and culture of his people.

Warri and Yatungka were deeply grieved at the loss of their friend. That they were still alive was due solely to Mudjon's insistence that a search be made for them and their needs ascertained.

In April 1979, Warri became ill and, despite treatment, died on 28 April. Yatungka, who had developed the same illness, was shattered by her husband's death. She was profoundly depressed, unable to accept the fact that the man she had eloped with, the man who had been by her side throughout those difficult years and who was her sole companion in recent times, was dead. She lost interest in life, she refused to take food and she joined Warri on 23 May 1979, less than four weeks after his death.

They, like Mudjon, were buried in the local cemetery, far from their homeland.

Perhaps we will never know whether they were happy at Wiluna. We do know, however, that they lived more than a year longer than if they had remained at Ngarinarri. They had been accepted by the elders once more, forgiven for their disregard of the law so long ago. I hope that in those months they lived amongst their people they did not pine for the desert, that the time that was left to them was enjoyable and comfortable.

We believe we were right in undertaking the search and bringing Warri and Yatungka out of the desert, and I pay tribute to two remarkable people of the Mandildjara, the last of the nomads.

The Last of His Tribe

He crouches, and buries his face on his knees,
　　And hides in the dark of his hair;
For he cannot look up to the storm-smitten trees,
　　Or think of the loneliness there:
　　　　Of the loss and the loneliness there.

The wallaroos grope through the tufts of the grass,
　　And turn to their covers for fear;
But he sits in the ashes and lets them pass
　　Where the boomerangs sleep with the spear:
　　　　With the nullah, the sling, and the spear.

Uloola, behold him! The thunder that breaks
　　On the tops of the rocks with the rain,
And the wind which drives up with the salt of the lakes,
　　Have made him a hunter again:
　　　　A hunter and fisher again.

For his eyes have been full with a smouldering thought;
　　But he dreams of the hunts of yore,
And of foes that he sought, and of fights that he fought
　　With those who will battle no more:
　　　　Who will go to the battle no more.

It is well that the water which tumbles and fills
    Goes moaning and moaning along;
For an echo rolls out from the sides of the hills,
    And he starts at a wonderful song:
        At the sounds of a wonderful song.

And he sees, through the rents of the scattering fogs,
    The corroboree warlike and grim,
And the lubra who sat by the fire on the logs,
    To watch, like a mourner, for him:
        Like a mother and mourner, for him.

Will he go in his sleep from these desolate lands,
    Like a chief, to the rest of his race,
With the honey-voiced woman who beckons, and stands,
    And gleams like a Dream in his face —
        Like a marvellous Dream in his face?

                                        Henry Kendall

Postscript, 2006

Nearly thirty years have passed since that dramatic moment when I, and my companions, stood on the crest of the sand ridge and saw the distant figure moving slowly across the spinifex plain. That moment heralded the end of the isolation and the struggle for existence of the last of the nomads in the Little Sandy and Gibson deserts.

Over the years since that time I have often thought of Warri and Yatungka, for the long search for them under the guidance of Mudjon and our meeting with them was one of the most moving episodes in my life.

That the story of the nomads struck a chord with readers in Australia and abroad is evident from the continued demand for *The Last of the Nomads*, which has been reprinted numerous times. That two elderly Aboriginal people continued to live in their country, enduring untold hardships in the late 1970s seemed to evoke great sympathy and even affection from many people. Because Warri and Yatungka had broken the laws of their people and chose to live deep in the desert where they could remain together rather than join their fellows and face retribution and separation, their life has been described as a wonderful love story of the desert. That they remained inseparable after they came out of the desert and Yatungka no longer wished to live after the death of Warri, adds some credence to that description.

The interest that has been generated by the book, and later the television documentary, nationally and internationally, has in fact been so great that in recent years there have been many visitors to the site where the Aboriginal couple were found, and there are now 'The Last of the Nomads Tours' which retrace the route that we took during our search.

Over the years I have had an increasing desire to return to the desert and retrace the route we took nearly thirty years ago, to visit the rock holes and soaks and, finally, to stand on that sand ridge and look out over the plain where Warri was first seen.

Since *The Last of the Nomads* was published in 1983, several film companies had expressed their desire to make a film of the story which they regarded as being of considerable interest and which would have a wide appeal, both in Australia and overseas. However, funding for such a project proved difficult to obtain and the idea had to be abandoned until 1996, when one film company was eventually successful and plans were made for a film of around one hour's duration.

Shooting was to begin in mid 1996, but I was unable to be involved at that time as 1996 was the centenary year of David Carnegie's epic journey from Coolgardie to Halls Creek. It had long been my ambition to retrace that journey using camels and it was imperative that I leave Coolgardie on 9 July, exactly one hundred years to the day that Carnegie and his party set out.

I anticipated that I would be on the move with my party and the camels for about three months and therefore would not be involved in any filming until October. This caused some concern, for the film company, having obtained funding, wished to proceed as soon as possible, wanting to complete their work and be out of the desert before the onset of hot weather. However, I could not alter my plans and consequently a tentative date to begin filming was made for 10 October, but this was dependant on my reaching my destination before then, and there were many who expressed doubts that I would have completed the long trek across the Gibson and Great Sandy deserts by that time or, indeed, whether I would complete it at all.

To the great relief of all concerned, I arrived in Halls Creek in late September and was ready to depart on the appointed date but, at the last moment, it was discovered that the area that we would be visiting was the subject of a Native Title claim. It was then necessary to postpone our departure and to arrange a meeting with the Aboriginal people concerned. We flew north to a rendezvous in the bed of the Oakover River where an agreement was reached whereby several Aboriginal people from the Port Hedland and Wiluna areas would accompany us through the desert during the filming to ensure that we did not film places and objects that were of a secret-sacred nature to their people.

We left Perth nine days later than originally planned and met the two groups of Aboriginal people in the Durba Hills on the Canning Stock Route. This was the place twenty years earlier where we took on our final supplies of water and from where our search for the nomads began. From that point Mudjon had been our guide and we travelled in any direction he wished to go for he was familiar with the country ahead, and he alone was the one who would locate the old Aboriginal couple if they were still alive.

After completing filming around the Durba Hills and Lake Disappointment we moved to Ngundrayo. As I walked up the gorge towards the spring I thought of that time long ago when I trod the same path with Mudjon, and I recalled his excitement when he located the water at the top of the gorge. It is fitting that the gorge is now named Mudjon Gorge, a tribute to a very remarkable Aboriginal man.

From Ngundrayo we travelled to Moongooloo and then went south-east, visiting the various rock holes and soaks where Mudjon had led us during the long search. It was at Walloogoobal rock hole that we first found evidence of the nomads, the footprints in the sand. They, of course, have long since disappeared, as has all other evidence of Warri and Yatungka's occupation of that place, but the Warrida stone still stands as it has done for thousands of years. But today there is nobody left to pay their respects. Walloogoobal was dry twenty years earlier but now it contained water, much to the delight of our Aboriginal companions who replenished their supplies there.

At Kata Kata well there was a poignant reminder of the nomads. The remains of the crude shelter under which they had sought refuge from the heat was still visible. It was at our camp a short distance south of the well that Mudjon had finally concluded that Warri and Yatungka had not survived. He had reached that view because there had been no reply to his 'smokes,' and because he believed the emaciated dingo that came in to our camp to have once belonged to the nomads.

As I looked up to the northern face of Kata Kata hill I thought of Mudjon who, after sending up a smoke, had climbed to the top and had spent a long time there searching the horizon for the reply which never came. Dispirited, as he descended after dusk he lit small fires on the hillside creating the impression that Aboriginal people were once more sitting around their camp fires on Kata Kata.

From Kata Kata we followed the chain of rock holes that finally led us to Ngarinarri. It was a very moving occasion to once more stand on the crest of the sand ridge and look across that plain to where Warri had first been seen. However, now there was nothing moving out there except the tall stalks of the spinifex wafting in the breeze. All human activity had ended twenty years earlier.

On Ngarinarri claypan the soak, which had been kept open by Aboriginal people for hundreds, and possibly thousands, of years was now silted up, and a large bush growing from it. This was the soak on which the nomads depended and from where Yatungka had been able to scrape enough water to barely keep them alive.

The cairn that we erected on the southern edge of the claypan as a memorial to Warri and Yatungka was still in position; the attached plaque announcing to any who might visit the place that it was there that the last of the nomads had lived during their last days or weeks in the desert.

Our filming was largely finished at Ngarinarri. My return to the desert had been completed. It had been an intensely interesting but sad journey across the country that had once been trodden by Aboriginal people as they moved from one rock hole to another but is now devoid of any human beings.

The final act was to visit the cemetery at Wiluna and pay my respects at the graves of Mudjon and two remarkable people, the last of the nomads.

Few of the graves in the Aboriginal portion of the Wiluna Cemetery have headstones to indicate who lies beneath, the graves being identified only by a number. In 2000, I and three companions, travelled to Wiluna to erect headstones and fences around the graves of the nomadic couple and our guide during the search. Soil that had been collected from their last campsite was placed under the headstones, and the inscription on the headstones reads:

WARRI KYANGO
DIED APRIL 28, 1979
AGED 70 YEARS
THE LAST OF THE NOMADS

YADOONGA (YATUNGKA) KYANGO
DIED MAY 23, 1979
AGED 62 YEARS
THE LAST OF THE NOMADS

FREDDY FREDDY
(MUDJON)
DIED JUNE 11, 1978
AGED 72 YEARS
A REMARKABLE MAN

Acknowledgements

I wish to express my gratitude to my companions on the journey, for without their enthusiasm and their ability to overcome the difficulties we encountered there would have been no story to relate. To Stan Gratte and Harry Lever, with whom I had ventured into the desert on previous occasions, I offer my thanks. To Stan, for his great interest in the desert and his knowledge of the country; to Harry, for his doggedness and for the culinary delights he always managed to serve, often under trying conditions.

To my colleague, John Hanrahan, my thanks for his companionship and the comfort of his Range Rover. I deeply appreciate his sense of history, his feeling for the Aboriginal people and his concern for the environment.

My thanks to Mark Whittome, who took every difficulty in his stride, and, above all, I express my gratitude to my great Aboriginal friend, Mudjon, for his companionship and guidance during our weeks together in the desert when he taught me so much about his 'country' and his people.

I would like to thank Henry and Mrs Ward, of Glenayle Station for their kindness and hospitality, and to the radio operators at the Royal Flying Doctor Base at Meekatharra I would also like to give thanks for their interest in our expedition and their assistance in maintaining contact with the outside world. To Mrs Crossland of Nedlands, my thanks for typing the manuscript, and to Ray Coffey and the Fremantle Arts Centre Press who considered that the story should be published my gratitude also. Finally I thank my wife, Anne, and my family for understanding one who needs, at times, to breathe the clear air of the desert, to wander his native land and to commune with nature.

Rarely in one's life does the opportunity arise to participate in a venture such as the journey we embarked upon, a seemingly hopeless search for the last of a people. That it met with success was due to the single-mindedness of all concerned, and the sight of that wisp of smoke rising above the sandhills of the Gibson Desert indicating that the last nomads had somehow managed to survive against appalling conditions of drought, was one of the most dramatic moments of my life and one I shall never forget.

This edition first published 2006 by
FREMANTLE PRESS
25 Quarry Street (PO Box 158), North Fremantle
Western Australia 6159.
www.fremantlepress.com.au

Reprinted 2009

First published 1983. Reprinted 1983, 1990, 1997, 2002.
Copyright © W J Peasley, 1983.

Cover designed by Allyson Crimp.
Typeset by Fremantle Arts Centre Press
and printed by Everbest Printing Co, China.

National Library of Australia
Cataloguing-in-publication data

Peasley, W J (William John), 1927 –.
The last of the nomads.

ISBN 9780949 206879.

1. Mandjildjara (Australian people). [2]. Aborigines — Australian —
Western Australia — Social life and customs. 3. Gibson Desert (WA) —
Description and travel. I. Title.

994.1009915